T0311466

Cambridge Elements ≡

Elements in Economics of European Integration
edited by
Nauro F. Campos
University College London

EUROPE AND THE TRANSFORMATION OF THE IRISH ECONOMY

John FitzGerald
Trinity College Dublin

Patrick Honohan
Peterson Institute for International Economics

Shaftesbury Road, Cambridge CB2 8EA, United Kingdom

One Liberty Plaza, 20th Floor, New York, NY 10006, USA

477 Williamstown Road, Port Melbourne, VIC 3207, Australia

314–321, 3rd Floor, Plot 3, Splendor Forum, Jasola District Centre,
New Delhi – 110025, India

103 Penang Road, #05–06/07, Visioncrest Commercial, Singapore 238467

Cambridge University Press is part of Cambridge University Press & Assessment,
a department of the University of Cambridge.

We share the University's mission to contribute to society through the pursuit of
education, learning and research at the highest international levels of excellence.

www.cambridge.org
Information on this title: www.cambridge.org/9781009306089

DOI: 10.1017/9781009306102

First published 2023

A catalogue record for this publication is available from the British Library.

ISBN 978-1-009-30608-9 Paperback
ISSN 2634-0763 (online)
ISSN 2634-0755 (print)

Europe and the Transformation of the Irish Economy

Elements in Economics of European Integration

DOI: 10.1017/9781009306102
First published online: May 2023

John FitzGerald
Trinity College Dublin

Patrick Honohan
Peterson Institute for International Economics

Author for correspondence: Patrick Honohan, patrick.honohan@gmail.com

Abstract: Having stagnated for decades in the shadow of the UK, the Irish economy's performance improved after it joined the European Union (EEC) in 1973. This Element shows how the challenge of EU membership gave focus and direction to Irish economic policy. No longer dependent on low value-added agricultural exports to Britain, within the EU Ireland became a hub for multinational corporations in IT and pharmaceutical products. This export success required and facilitated a strengthening of education and social policy infrastructures, and underpinned the achievement of high average living standards. EU membership has also brought challenges, and several severe setbacks have resulted from Irish policy mistakes. But the European flavour of Ireland's structural policies (leavened with exposure to US experience) has helped it navigate the hazards of hyper-globalization with fewer political tensions than seen elsewhere.

Keywords: Irish economic policy, European Union, tax competition, Euro crisis, economic growth

JEL classifications: F63, N14, N34, O52.

ISBNs: 9781009306089 (PB), 9781009306102 (OC)
ISSNs: 2634-0763 (online), 2634-0755 (print)

Contents

1 Introduction

Despite the setbacks of the financial crisis and the pandemic, the last several decades have seen economic prosperity in Ireland make advances that seemed impossible half a century ago. This has also been the period of Ireland's membership of the European Union,[1] and it followed a long period of stagnation in the shadow of its large neighbour and former ruler, the United Kingdom.

Exactly where the turning point in Ireland's economic fortunes was, and what role EU membership played, are less clear. Population started to grow from 1961; productivity from the early 1970s; per capita consumption levels in the late 1980s; employment growth in the 1990s (Figure 1) (Honohan and Walsh 2002; Ó Gráda and O'Rourke 2022; O'Rourke 2017).

This book explores the ways in which the deepening relationship with Europe influenced the extent, nature and timing of the economic transformation.

The four freedoms of movement within the Union – of goods and services, of people and of capital – are all ingredients in the story of this transformation, which has happened in an environment significantly shaped by EU economic legislation.

But arguably more important has been the way in which joining the EU catalysed a much larger opening up of the Irish economy to the opportunities of an increasingly globalized world.

Free Trade in Goods and Services and the Transformation of the Business Sector

The Irish policymakers who advocated membership more than sixty years ago saw progress to free trade with Europe as crucial in expanding the market for Irish agriculture and industry. Agriculture clearly benefitted from the high prices secured at the outset, and there was an expectation that value added processing of agricultural products would drive industrial expansion. Removing the barriers to trade would force Irish firms to improve efficiency to compete with British and continental firms. But many of the old firms did not long survive.

Instead, inward foreign direct investment by firms that would supply both the European and other foreign markets, encouraged by grants, and especially by low rates of corporation profits tax, proved to be the distinctive characteristic of Ireland's industrial modernization.

---

[1] Although called this only from 1993, the term European Union (EU) will frequently be used for convenience for the Union's predecessors, Common Market, EEC, etc. Except where stated explicitly, Ireland refers to the Republic.

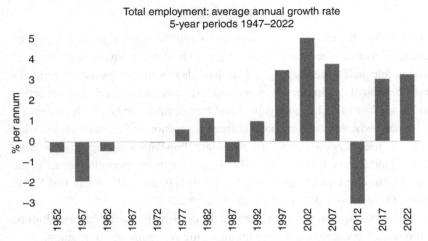

Figure 1 Total employment annual growth rates (five-year averages)
Source: Central Statistics Office.

The European Single Market, unleashed at the start of 1993, greatly deepened the process of European trade integration and increased the attraction of Ireland as an export platform for foreign-owned firms. Already an especially favoured destination for US foreign direct investment (FDI), Ireland experienced a disproportionate inflow in the 1990s as the Single Market came into effect, helping drive a delayed convergence towards the prosperity of leading economies.

Free access to the European market turned out to be only a part of the benefit of this globalization of production, though, as new firms increasingly supplied a world market. FDI featured new fields of production such as information services, information technology, medical instruments and pharmaceuticals.

Conventional accounting practice generates statistics on output, trade and productivity that overstate the true performance in Ireland of the world's major technology and pharmaceutical companies. Still, over the last fifty years FDI has made a major contribution to rising living standards in the form of growing employment, tax revenue and know-how. The multinational corporations (MNCs) did not create the Celtic Tiger of the 1990s, but their growth was a significant part of it. They did not provide much insulation of the economy from the Global Financial Crisis (GFC), but they greatly helped strengthen the public finances through the pandemic years 2020–2.

In time, new or growing Irish-owned firms in such fields as agribusiness, building materials and air transport also became firmly established internationally, and again these took full advantage of the globalized world economy, and not just Europe.

Key Pre-requisites: Education and Macroeconomic Stability

Translating this transformation of productive forces into broad-based and sustained prosperity called for steps that lay largely in the hands of the national government, rather than with the EU. Arguably the two most important of these were education and macroeconomic stability.

In the 1960s, Government belatedly recognized that Ireland had fallen well behind in ensuring access to education at second and third levels. Measures were taken to correct this and to catch up with what had been happening in other European countries.

There was less success in the matter of macroeconomic stability. Fiscal policy mistakes following the oil price rises of the 1970s led to a loss of competitiveness, and a debt overhang which resulted in a deep macroeconomic crisis for most of the 1980s. This delayed convergence of the economy to its full employment potential.

Thus it was only by the end of the 1980s that both of these key ingredients were in place. Ireland then experienced two decades of rapid economic catch-up towards the living standards of the leading group of EU countries.

Capital Mobility and Crises

The benign environment created by the Single European Market, and by falling transportation and communications costs, ushered in the 'Celtic Tiger' period of export-led employment growth. Competitive and productive, the business sector at last ended the involuntary joblessness that had been endemic.

But, as the new millennium began, Government again allowed macroeconomic imbalances, associated with reckless and under-supervised banking, to re-emerge in the later years of the catch-up, leaving Ireland disastrously exposed to the GFC.

Freedom of mobile capital thus proved to be a mixed blessing, as these episodes of macroeconomic imbalance interacted with speculative capital flows from global financial markets to deepen the two severe macroeconomic crises. Neither of the two European currency arrangements in place during the two Irish macroeconomic crises provided much protection to Irish economic performance.

European financial architecture was not sufficiently developed to help: it was not until the 1990s that the Union started to pay attention to fiscal imbalances, and not until after the GFC that it centralized banking supervision. Whether enough has been done to ensure that the latest macroeconomic shocks are weathered remains to be seen.

Labour Mobility

Much of the sizable immigration of the last few decades has been from the new wave of EU member states after 2004, reflecting the EU freedom of personal movement. Population growth since 1961 was also boosted by returning migrants. In contrast, only a small proportion of Irish emigrants chose destinations in Continental Europe.

Armed with more years of education, the workforce was more productive, and the share of the population at work outside of agriculture grew rapidly in the decades of EU membership, with far more women participating than before, especially those who benefitted from the expansion of second- and third-level education. Elements of European social policy played a role here, for example on equal pay for women, and likely influenced Irish policies that helped limit the deterioration in income inequality.

Funding and Regulations from Europe

The Structural Funds made a considerable contribution to Irish economic progress in the 1990s (as the transfers associated with the Common Agricultural Policy had been doing from the start). Their expansion arrived at an ideal moment, encouraging the relaunching of many needed infrastructural and other Government spending programmes that had been deferred as the fiscal accounts were being repaired. The funds were well spent, and the governance of the spending helped improve Irish administrative processes.

Over a period during which public regulation of economic activity had to become more elaborate and prescriptive, Ireland's participation in the EU has helped ensure that its microeconomic policies reflect up-to-date international practice and are less prone to capture by sectional interests than might have been the case. Irish engagement in the design of these policies has varied, having been very active in respect of agriculture, for example, but notably weaker in environmental protection over the years. Restrictive practices in domestic service sectors such as the law persist.

Large areas of policy remain a national responsibility, though, and solutions to the many obvious deficiencies in fields such as healthcare, legal services and especially housing can only be sought at home.

There is a path-dependency in the story of Ireland's economic transformation which precludes any simple decomposition of the result into distinct contributions from each main causal factor: EU membership; stabilization policy; the openness to FDI and the low-tax approach to attracting it; investment in education; globalization and the European Single Market. For more than a decade after joining the EEC, the Irish economy was still in the doldrums, owing to macroeconomic mismanagement. But during that time, the investment in human capital and the arrival of the early waves of US MNCs were laying foundations of subsequent advances. Both of these ingredients were selected by policymakers whose awareness of international opportunities reflected an out-ward-looking attitude informed by personal links to the diaspora and growing professional and personal links to Continental Europe. Thanks to these founda-tions, the economy was uniquely well placed to benefit from globalization, and from the European Single Market which arrived soon after macroeconomic balance had been restored.

The remaining sections are organized as follows.

Section 2 focuses on how the freedom of trade in goods and services affected the modernization of Ireland's productive capacity. We emphasize how this was not confined to European links, but saw Ireland embracing globalization to a remarkable extent.

Section 3 is about people, ranging from the large immigration from Eastern Europe that has happened in recent years (thanks to the freedom of movement of people within the EU) to how educational attainment increased labour force participation and productivity, especially for women. It also discusses the distribution of income between households.

Section 4 looks at how Ireland's engagement with the microeconomic legis-lation and policies of the Union, and its Structural Funds, have influenced the extent and quality of economic growth.

Freedom of capital movement has been a mixed blessing for Ireland. Before concluding, Section 5 looks at Ireland's chequered macroeconomic policy experience within the EU, noting how mistakes slowed the convergence of living standards in the early years and again resulted in another serious setback during the GFC.

2 The Modernization of Production

A small economy can exploit the economies of scale available in modern production processes only through specialization and export. Maintaining bar-riers to international trade, whether inward and outward, will ultimately prevent this progression. That is why Irish policymakers saw membership of the European Common Market – and eventually the Single Market – as presenting more of an opportunity than a threat to Ireland over the past half century.

The efficiency and competitiveness of the Irish economy did improve, though not in quite the way that was expected. Rather than simply diversifying its exports into Continental Europe, Ireland built also on the cultural links with the United States to attract and build enterprises engaged in the global economy to an extent and in ways not conceived of sixty years ago. Instead of simply adding value to Ireland's traditional agricultural products (livestock, milk and eggs), production for exports swung into sectors such as pharmaceuticals, information and medical technology and software.

The role of Europe in this modernization was at first largely catalytic, in motivating the initial shift of policy, in opening new horizons, and in underpinning a stable regulatory framework on which entrepreneurs could build. Europe also provided an increasingly important market, especially when non-tariff barriers to trade were progressively removed as the Single Market process matured.

Of the four freedoms at the heart of the European Union, trade came first. As European countries recovered from the Second World War, the political as well as economic desirability of free trade re-asserted itself.

Sixty years ago Ireland was not well placed to benefit from this new trend towards free trade. Its agricultural and industrial structure had been formed in the shadow of the much larger British economy and was shaped by the trading opportunities that that provided. Furthermore, it had retained a high level of tariff protection from the interwar period: indeed rates of effective protection were among the highest in the world (McAleese 1971).

Thus, for example, the Anglo-Irish 'economic war' of the 1930s, which exacerbated the – then global – trend towards protection, reinforced a switch to import substitution, with the creation of numerous manufacturing firms in Ireland in sectors such as textiles, clothing, footwear and building materials. However their scale and efficiency were insufficient to allow them to compete internationally.

The top four principal export products from Ireland in 1949 were live cattle and horses, fresh eggs and beer, mainly sent to Britain. By the late 1950s, despite grant and tax advantages offered to firms to encourage exports, live animals and food, drink and tobacco still accounted for almost 70 per cent of Ireland's goods exports.

The limited employment and income-generating capacity of Irish economic activity had long resulted in a steady net migration outflow and population decline. With imports likely to make further inroads into the ability of inefficient Irish firms to stay in business, and agriculture offering no growth in employment, Irish policymakers of the 1950s concluded that the only way forward was to encourage a drive for efficiency in manufacturing production for export and that this would be helped by the encouragement of inward FDI. Manufacturing efficiency was not to be achieved behind protective tariffs.

The emergence of the two free-trade blocs (the European Free Trade Association EFTA as well as the European Economic Community EEC) made the international competitiveness of Irish industry an even more pressing matter. Together with global trends towards freeing of trade, competition in Ireland's traditional export market Britain, and in new markets, was going to be increasingly tough.

'It seems clear,' wrote the top official of the Department of Finance in 1958 (in a widely read report that was influential in shaping subsequent policy), 'that, sooner or later, protection will have to go and the challenge of free trade be accepted.'

And so it was. Ireland began to liberalize, signing, for example, a free trade area agreement with Britain in 1965, which would eliminate Irish tariffs on UK manufactures over a nine-year period, greatly increasing the competitive pressure on Irish firms producing for the domestic market. The agreement was explicitly portrayed as a stepping stone towards the rigours of EEC membership and was signed in the full knowledge that not every Irish manufacturer would survive. What concessions were made in this agreement on the British side mainly referred to agriculture, as most Irish manufactured exports to Britain were already tariff-free (Blackwell and O'Malley 1984; Daly 2016, p. 30).

Although Britain's 1961 application to join the European Economic Community was unsuccessful, implying that Ireland too would not join yet, Ireland's economic policies had turned definitively towards generating sufficient productive efficiency to compete successfully in Europe. With Ireland's per capita income less than two-thirds that of the original six member states, Ireland was not obviously well qualified to join the Common Market (Laffan 2021). Unless the efficiency and productivity of Irish industry could be raised, Ireland's economically underdeveloped status might impede admission, if and when Britain was eventually admitted. Irish industry would have to adapt, and there was a push for firms to rationalize and reach scale, including through mergers (Ó Gráda 1997). Many of the old firms did not successfully shape up, though, but gradually retreated.

Retreating Industries

Back in 1960, Ireland's industrial structure was dominated by firms producing for the domestic market. Some of these were subsidiaries of British firms that had entered to jump tariffs that began to be applied already in the 1920s. A further wave of firm creation had happened in the 1930s as tariffs and quotas became much tighter (Neary and Ó Gráda 1991; Ryan 1949); but more of the owners were local in this wave, reflecting legislation that curbed inward FDI. The result had been highly profitable for Irish owners of firms thus endowed with monopoly powers, whether through protection from import competition, or through being awarded import licenses. Some of these firms retained close British connections, despite the restrictive legislation.

There was a limit to the extent to which import substitution behind tariff walls could support the growth of firms. Manufacturing employment grew little after 1938, with the local market saturated and most of the firms unable to compete in international markets.

Just as Belfast had world-leading export firms in shipbuilding, linen and tobacco in the early decades of the twentieth century, Dublin did have the long-established brewing concern Guinness, and, on a smaller scale, the biscuit manufacturer Jacobs; and Cork the Ford tractor plant. But these and a few others were exceptions, and even they came under pressure from protection in Britain and competition from further afield (Bielenberg and Ryan 2016; Jacobson 1977).

Many of the old firms succumbed in the early years of free trade, especially during the recession of the mid-1970s and mid-1980s. Few managed to make the breakthrough to becoming successful exporters in the wider EU market now available to them. Weaknesses in management, marketing and design were widely cited as reasons; perhaps also (as Blackwell and O'Malley 1984 suggested) the set-up costs required to break into this market presented too high a barrier for the small firms that dominated the Irish industrial scene.

Some of the existing firms did modernize. For example, the three largest alcohol distilling firms merged into what became Irish Distillers, which did succeed in expanding the international market for Irish whiskey and other spirits, before being taken over by a French group. Guinness survived also – albeit as a division of the British group Diageo, with only about 1,200 employees now in Ireland – and it continues to brew stout for the UK market in Dublin. As discussed later, the important beef and milk processing sectors also modernized and consolidated, and a few of the merged firms were transformed into significant international firms with outward FDI.

In most cases, though, it was ultimately not a question of re-equipping and modernizing existing firms, but rather a process of replacement of failing firms, unable to survive without protection, by new entrants. The vehicle turned out to be inward foreign direct investment.

The Multinational Firms

Countries

Efforts in this direction already began in the early 1950s with the creation of the important promotion agency then known as the Industrial Development Authority (IDA), and its work expanded in the 1960s. At first the IDA managed to attract a number of significant German firms – their nationality partly reflecting a reluctance to see a return to British dominance, and partly the preference of some German entrepreneurs, needing access to labour, to locate in Ireland rather than in Britain (Daly 2016). Other prominent early arrivals in the 1970s included Italian, British and Japanese synthetic fibre plants. Soon, however, the main fruits of the IDA's promotional activity were coming from the United States.

By the mid-1970s, the IDA was attracting FDI flows on a disproportionate scale compared to the rest of Europe – though inflows slowed markedly during the 1980s, before recovering strongly thereafter. The share of foreign-owned firms in industrial employment grew rapidly, stabilizing only in the late 1990s (as indigenous enterprises expanded, including in the construction sector).

Being able to export into Europe without tariffs or quotas was, of course, an important part of what generated interest in an Irish location. But it would be a mistake to see this FDI as solely engaged in tariff jumping into Europe. Instead it should be noted that MNCs also exported a considerable fraction of their output to the United States and elsewhere.[2]

Through the early decades of the Community, considerable non-tariff barriers persisted in Europe, including those associated with home preference in government procurement and discriminatory national technical standards. The Single Market reforms of the 1980s dismantled many of these non-tariff barriers, thereby opening up additional opportunities especially in sectors which were now particularly well represented in Ireland, thanks to FDI (Barry et al. 1999).

Aside from the absence of a language barrier, the attractions emphasized by the IDA for these firms included not only location within the Common Market, but also sizable grant-aid, including (as emphasized by Crafts 2014) the relatively light degree of product market and labour market regulation, compared to other parts of the EU.

But increasingly important was the ability of many MNCs to exploit the low Irish rate of tax on corporate profits.

The tax rate gap relative to other European countries was considerable. Around the turn of the millennium, a typical new investment, if located in Ireland, could expect to pay in corporate taxes only a quarter of what it would have to pay in other euro area countries (Oxford University Centre for Business Taxation 2017). One international econometric study estimated that, if all EU countries had the same tax rate in the 1990s, the net inflow of FDI to Ireland

---

[2] Using regression analysis of detailed (4-digit) US import data by product, Romalis (2007) shows that Ireland's share in US imports tended to be higher for more capital-intensive sectors with lower trade costs.

would have been less than a third of what it was (Gropp and Kostial 2000; cf. Davies et al. 2021).

Because of the structure of US corporate taxation, the tax advantage was most attractive to large US-based multinational groups.[3]

US Firms

It was US firms that responded most strongly to the advantages and inducements to locate production facilities in Ireland. Already in 1975 they accounted for a quarter of employment in foreign-owned IDA supported firms, compared with 39 per cent in British companies, and 8 per cent German.[4] By 1995, the British share had fallen to 14 per cent with the US at 59 per cent. The share of firms from Continental Europe fell from 32 per cent to 24 per cent (Ruane and Görg 1997). After 1995, the growth in employment at US firms accelerated until the turn of the century, and again after 2012, until by 2020 they accounted for more than 70 per cent of the employment in foreign-owned firms in the corresponding sectors (i.e. those assisted by the IDA), with the UK now only accounting for 3 per cent and Continental Europe for about 11 per cent (cf. Brazys and Regan 2021).

In fact, Ireland has been a specially favoured destination for outward US FDI (Figure 1). Capital investment by US MNCs in Ireland, which averaged 5 per cent of GDP per annum between 1983 and 1995, was proportionately the highest of any EU country and about five times the average (Görg and Ruane 1999). Even Spain and Portugal, new members whose accession triggered an economic expansion in those years, experienced nothing like this inflow.

From 1993 US firms saw new advantage in having a production location within the Single Market. FDI flows from the US increased in the following years, and Ireland increased its share of those flows (Görg and Ruane 1999; Jacobson and Andreosso 1990). By 2019 US MNCs paid more corporate income tax to Ireland than to any other foreign jurisdiction, other than the UK (and that country was only slightly ahead) and, relative to population, more people work for US MNCs in Ireland than elsewhere.

Clearly, EU membership did not guarantee what happened in respect of inward US investment to Ireland. Ireland's experience in attracting US investment was quite unique, as illustrated in Figure 2, which shows the share of total employment in EU countries provided by foreign firms from different regions.

---

[3] For example, the profit rate of German firms in Ireland is not out of line with Irish firms, or with the profit rate in their home market, suggesting that they have little scope to reduce their overall taxation by locating profits in Ireland (FitzGerald 2022a).

[4] The industrial development agencies maintain a database of the firms supported by their activities. This does not include all foreign-owned firms, such as supermarket chains; on the other hand, it is not limited to 'newly arriving' firms.

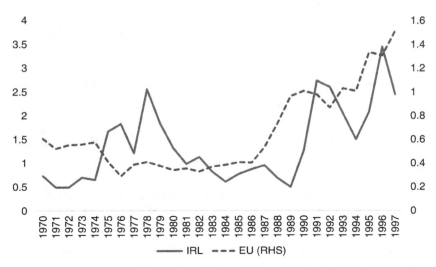

Figure 2 Foreign direct investment inflows, EU and Ireland, 1970–97, % GDP
Source: World Bank World Development Indicators.

This seems to be the result of a combination of favourable factors: the deliberate and successful official efforts, through the IDA, to attract US FDI, relying to some extent on the deep cultural and historic links between Ireland and the United States; and the credibility and stability of the tax advantage.

Manufacturing Sectors

The IDA trawled widely across sectors for likely investors, often drawing on Irish-American business networks, and sometimes attracting firms not likely to have a long life in a prospering economy because of their dependence on low labour costs. An extreme example was a clothing manufacturer, Fruit of the Loom, which arrived in 1987 and, at its peak, employed more than 3,500 people on the island. It was inevitable that this firm would offer limited prospects for high wages, and that, as Irish wages increased, it would soon be undercut by exports from emerging markets; eventually it was wound down in the 2000s, with production moved to Morocco.

Thus the industrial sectors in which foreign ownership had first been most prominent quickly lost their dominance. In 1975, over a quarter of employment in foreign-owned industry had been in the food, drink and tobacco sectors, and more than a sixth in textiles, clothing and footwear; these percentages declined sharply over the following years reaching just 11 and 3 per cent, respectively, by the end of the century (Barry 2007). Indeed, as early as 1972, inward FDI had begun to concentrate on sectors sought out as appropriate to a geographically

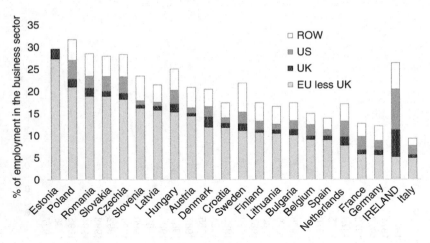

Figure 3 Employment in the business sector, EU countries 2019. By nationality of the controllers of the businesses

Source: Eurostat.

peripheral economy because of their low weight-to-value ratio products such as electrical devices and pharmaceuticals (MacSharry and White 2000, p. 207). Soon software products and pharmaceuticals became the most conspicuous of the new tax-advantaged manufacturing sectors. For these two sectors, net output per employee in Ireland in 1999 was 11 times (software) and 5 times (pharmaceuticals) the average for the same sectors in the rest of the EU. Another sector, dominated by cola concentrates, also gave a ratio in excess of 11, and only somewhat less exceptional were the net output figures for computers and electronic components. Clearly, the enormously high output value per worker in these sectors reflected the relevant firms' past investment in physical and especially intellectual capital. No doubt a considerable amount of transfer pricing (in transactions between different units of each multinational group) underlay such differences, arranged to ensure that the return on this investment was attached to the group's unit in the low-tax jurisdiction. With the wage bill such a small fraction of net output, these firms were highly profitable – though the ultimate source of these profits was typically the proprietary knowledge and distribution network of the US-based parents (Honohan and Walsh 2002).

If electronics, computer software, biotechnology and healthcare products were, by 1983, being trumpeted by the IDA as the sectors of its focus, this peculiar, but lucky, sectoral skew of inward FDI to high-tech industries was not something that had been specifically incentivized by EU policy. The association with science-based industries did prove to be fortunate, as these were sectors whose long-term growth potential was to be amply fulfilled, as was their ability to weather recessions better than many other sectors. And the science-based approach percolated through the economy: research and development personnel now account for a higher proportion of employment in Ireland than in most other advanced economies.

But for the large high-tech foreign-owned MNCs, the underlying research and development work was largely done abroad: their Irish establishments were mainly production facilities (O'Leary 2015). Indeed, for many years the design of the tax incentives actually discouraged firms from locating cost centres such as R&D in Ireland. Profits generated from these activities are nevertheless booked to the Irish establishments and remitted to affiliates abroad creating very notable distortions in the national balance of payments statistics. In other cases huge royalties were paid for the use of patents.

Services

Inward FDI also expanded into internationally traded services, including financial services, as this one of the four freedoms of European integration became better established.

Special legislation created Dublin's International Financial Services Centre (IFSC) in 1987, a tax-advantaged location for export-oriented financial services. By 2020 IFSC companies employed about 38,000 persons and were a significant source of tax revenue. Ranked 15 in the world among offshore financial centres, the IFSC became a leading home of US dollar-based investment funds and of certain specialized insurance products, most of which could be passported into the rest of the EU. Half-a-dozen of the world's largest banks built a significant presence, each employing thousands in Ireland. Some, though not all, of these financial service companies required authorization and supervision by the Central Bank, which until 2010 had the statutory function of promoting the development of the financial services industry. There were suggestions in the early 2000s that some incoming financial services firms were motivated by regulatory arbitrage as well as by the tax advantages, but such complaints were not heard in the years following the financial crisis of 2008–13.

Benefitting from specific features of the Irish tax code, several of the world's largest international aircraft leasing companies, starting with the Irish-controlled firm GPA, established their headquarters in Ireland. Between them they now own thousands of airliners which are leased to airlines all over the world. Almost all of their equity and debt is held outside the State, but they do have a highly skilled, albeit very small, Irish workforce – the leading firms employ only about one person in Ireland for every three airliners owned.

While taxation was a significant factor in locating in Ireland, and although the wage bills of many of these large tax-motivated service firms was a small component of their net output in Ireland, these were not empty shell operations. The top four US-based information and communications firms alone had between them well over 20,000 employees in Ireland in 2022 – almost 1 per cent of total employment.

The provision of key business services to the MNCs located in Ireland forms a significant part of the revenue stream of the largest Irish legal and accounting firms.

Measurement Puzzles

The exploitation of many complex features in Irish tax by some US, and latterly UK, companies, among others, has continued to grow. To this day, analysts struggle to make sense of the distortions these and other practices introduce into Irish economic statistics. Indeed, the scale of financial flows generated by these tax avoidance arrangements through Ireland is relevant in global statistics (cf. Tørsløv et al. 2022), and they have become increasingly controversial at a political level especially in the EU (see Section 4).

In effect, a large portion of the activities of some of the largest firms in the world are booked to their Irish affiliates. Export data is thereby boosted, though much of the receipts will flow out again in profit remittances. Data on the level and growth of industrial productivity cannot be compared with that of a typical country.

Even pinning down the nationality of firms has become difficult. For example, a number of foreign-controlled firms have found it advantageous to invert their ownership structures so that an Irish-domiciled firm has become the group's parent, even though most of the group's business is abroad. Listings of the largest Irish-domiciled firms now include several of these inversions.

For the analyst of Ireland's economic performance, these distortions have made key macroeconomic indicators, including GDP, exports and productivity meaningless unless modified. In the 1980s substituting GNI for GDP was a sufficient adjustment for aggregate income, since it stripped out profits attributed to non-resident firms. But in recent decades the corporate structures devised to optimize use of the tax code mean that this adjustment is not enough, especially when some large firms began to move much of their intellectual property to the ownership of their Irish affiliates. In order to avoid the contamination of GNI by tax-driven MNC accounting, Irish economists now use a new series called modified GNI or GNI* in making international comparisons with the GNI of other countries.[5]

---

[5] Depreciation on the intellectual property of MNCs and on leased aircraft are excluded from GNI*, as are the profits of some corporate inversions ('re-domiciled PLCs'). Cf. Economic Statistics Review Group (2016).

Still, the contribution of the MNCs to employment and tax revenue should not be understated. While reducing their global tax liability, these firms have generated sizable tax revenue for Ireland, especially since 2015.[6] Taking all foreign-owned companies together, thus including non-grant-aided firms in sectors such as retailing, MNCs account for a little over half of all the main taxes (corporation tax, income taxes in respect of their employees, value added tax) that are paid by firms in Ireland. This tax share and the comparable employment share are perhaps the best simple summary of the true scale of the foreign business sector (and less distorted than the larger shares obtained from export or production statistics).[7]

Indigenous Firms

Those who sought to attract inward FDI hoped from the outset that linkages and spill-overs would be important, and that Irish suppliers would emerge or grow to meet the demand from the MNCs. With the exception of agricultural inputs (discussed herein) this did not at first materialize to any great extent (Ruane and Uğur 2010). Another hope was that many Irish employees of the foreign-owned companies would gain sufficient experience to set up on their own; that many Irish start-ups would thus be spawned by the mere presence of MNCs and that some of these would attain scale and efficiency that could allow them to penetrate foreign markets. Here there were some results, though the process was gradual, and in many cases successful Irish graduates of MNC management moved instead to the UK or the US and made their entrepreneurial marks there.

Yet a number of local firms, some of them start-ups, and some built on a longer foundation, did grow in the years after membership, with the ambition to become major international players. Not all succeeded, and indeed Ireland in the 1980s and 1990s saw more than its fair share of relatively large corporate failures among such firms. A look at some of the successes and failures among larger firms provides an instructive view of the kinds of dynamic that affected Irish firms more widely.

Perhaps surprisingly, the most conspicuous of these large indigenous firms operated in fields other than the information technology and pharmaceuticals sectors that were growing so successfully under foreign ownership. Several highly successful service sector firms, like the budget airline Ryanair, the betting concern Paddy Power and the medical trials firm ICON, were founded in Ireland in the mid-to-late 1980s, and retained a significant presence in Ireland

---

[6] By 2021 the corporation tax paid by just ten foreign-owned firms accounted for more 11 per cent of Ireland's total tax revenue – contributing to fiscal vulnerability as mentioned in Section 5).

[7] Indeed, in the years of post-financial crisis recovery, agency-supported foreign-owned firms added almost a fifth of the total increase in employment in the economy as a whole.

as they expanded internationally both organically and through acquisition. Of these, Ryanair has been easily the most successful, and the most European, growing as it did to become the largest airline in Europe. A dramatic reduction in the cost of air transport to and from Ireland was an important consequence of Ryanair's market entry.

Equally distant from the main inward FDI sectors, the packaging specialist Smurfit Kappa employs about 45,000 people in 35 countries. Its origins date back to the 1930s, but, following consolidation through merger in the Irish market, its international footprint grew rapidly from the 1970s through acquisition first in Britain, then in the United States, Europe and Latin America. Nowadays Smurfit Kappa's employment, production and sales presence in Ireland are a small part of its total.

CRH, with 77,000 workers worldwide producing cement and other construction materials, is another indigenous firm with origins dating to the first half of the twentieth century. After the two leading construction materials firms, Cement and Roadstone, merged in 1970, the company embarked on international expansion through acquisition first in Europe and then in the United States to the point where it claims to be the largest construction materials concern in both markets.

The common thread in the story of Smurfit and CRH is that they first achieved scale at the national level through merger in the years running up to EU membership and used this base as the springboard for international expansion not confined to Europe, but also with an important focus on the United States. Notably, though, they also relied heavily on production facilities abroad (in the countries into which they were selling), reflecting the fact that they were specialized in products less accessible to international trade (cf. Görg 2000).

These were not the only significant firms to follow this route successfully. As mentioned earlier, Irish Distillers also followed this successful model of merging and expanding to supply a global market.

Thus the horizons of successful Irish businesses were broadening beyond Britain and were not confined to the EU market. The effectiveness of these firms naturally puts paid to old ideas that Ireland lacked entrepreneurs or could not achieve productive efficiencies. The business model of these firms also requires a high ability to work across cultural divides as they integrate operations in multiple countries. This was not the picture of Irish business that had been painted by a Committee on Industrial Organization in 1962, assessing the prospects for Irish industry in the coming free trade environment. That Committee had complained about short production lines, low productivity, poor training, absence of budgetary and stock controls, and shortcomings in marketing and management. Nor was it the picture painted by the Telesis

Consulting firm in a report prepared for the Irish Government in 1982 which had bemoaned the insufficient involvement of large indigenous firms in traded or skilled sub-supply industries.

At least the leading firms had overcome many of these deficiencies, rising to the challenge of free trade, and perhaps also benefitting from observation of the operating practices of the incoming firms from the US and Germany, including by former employees of the MNCs.

Combining consolidation, scale and international expansion was not a sure-fire recipe for success. Many of the larger indigenous firms, despite thrusting efforts, failed to survive (Cahill 1997). The most interesting of these failures was the aircraft leasing company GPA, founded in 1975, which had expanded rapidly on the basis of tax-advantaged debt finance sourced mainly from Japanese and other international banks. By 1992 it owned 315 aircraft, and managed a further 409. At that point it decided to raise additional equity to achieve an improved financial structure relative to what was beginning to seem overleveraged. The ability of GPA to support the debts it had assumed depended on continuing rapid growth in the demand for air travel. Market scepticism resulted in the proposed IPO failing, which caused market confidence in the firm to collapse more generally, leading to a downward financial spiral which saw its assets disposed of and most of its 317 employees dispersed. Another Irish transport firm that failed due to excessive leverage based on over-optimistic transportation demand projections was the State-owned Irish Shipping, which collapsed in 1984. The decision of the Government not to pay the creditors of this firm (mostly Japanese ship-owners and financiers), but to allow the liquidation to proceed, reflected the fiscal pressures of the time (discussed in Section 5).

Yet, the GPA model had not been all wrong, and the large foreign-controlled leasing firms that now operate successfully out of Irish headquarters (mentioned above) all drew inspiration – and many of their key staff – from GPA. Once again, though, these firms tend to serve a global market of which Europe accounts for little more than a quarter.

Other long-established Irish firms that failed to thrive, despite systematic efforts to grow internationally, included the tobacco concern P.J. Carroll, dating back to 1824, and Waterford Glass, a firm whose post-war re-establishment built on a long – albeit somewhat tenuous – tradition of glass making in that city. Carroll's attempts in the 1970s and 1980s to pivot from a declining core business into totally unrelated activities (including fish farming and manufacture of towels) were unsuccessful. Waterford sought to expand into a cognate sector by acquiring the British pottery concern Wedgwood, but this was not ultimately a success and the group failed in 2009.

Irish financial service firms also consolidated through merger in the 1960s. The leading firms chafed at the limitations of the small Irish market, but their attempts to enter the US market in the 1980s misfired. A new wave of expansion in the early 2000s, which included a big acquisition in Poland by the largest Irish bank, but was concentrated on lending to Irish property developers, ended disastrously with the effective failure of all of the significant banks in Ireland in the crisis of 2008–9 (discussed in Section 5), with the main ones rescued by the State or by their foreign shareholders. The insurance sector was marred by a sequence of major failures over the years attributable to reckless under-pricing, over-trading and, in the case of the Quinn Group, misuse of policy-holder funds.

Faced with untrammelled competition from the rest of the EU, Irish producers who were focused on the domestic market also had to up their game if they were to survive. They too could learn from the management practices of the successful FDI arrivals. Nevertheless, in the domestic market also, foreign-owned firms played a sizable role. Even in retailing, though there have been notable local successes, such as the discount clothing firm Primark (itself part of a British group, but managed from Ireland), British retailers retain an important market share.

Although overshadowed by the spectacular growth of MNCs in Ireland, this mixed experience of leading firms is mirrored throughout Irish industry. There are many smaller firms that were and are successful, including in the new sectors, and many that failed.

Agriculture and Agribusiness

Among the successes were several large food companies which did eventually fulfil the expectation of the late 1950s that free trade offered important potential for adding value to Ireland's agricultural production.

Agriculture is the sector that was most conspicuously and immediately affected by EU membership, which produced a big increase in agricultural product prices. Admittedly, some of the higher prices for agricultural products were in effect paid by Irish consumers. On the other hand, the CAP support mechanisms meant that farm incomes could be supported without drawing on the government's budget, as in the past.

The European price supports offered opportunities for profitable expansion. Farmers responded to the various price trends, building animal herds, choosing new breeds optimized for the new market conditions and building automated milking facilities. Beef and milk, strongly supported by EU Common Agricultural Policy (CAP) mechanisms, retained their dominant historical position. Boosted by the subsidies of the CAP, these products could now find their way to a wider global market.

Cattle numbers peaked in 1974 having risen by more than 50 per cent in the previous decade and a half, with the increase disproportionately favouring dairy cows, reflecting the particularly strong price increase for milk. Production of cattle, pigs, sheep and horses also remained important.

This expansion in production was accompanied by increasing concentration and declining employment in agriculture. The growing scale and professionalism of the leading farms, especially in dairying, meant a decline of almost 90 per cent in the number of dairy herds since the late 1960s, despite the increase in output. Overall, the number of agricultural holdings fell by almost a half in the first twenty years of EU membership. Mechanization meant that the increased scale could be managed with a smaller number of workers, and soon almost all the labour input on the farm came from the farm family (O'Donoghue 2022). By the early years of the new millennium, agriculture's share of total employment, which had been 35 per cent in 1961, had fallen to 5 per cent.

The introduction in 1984 of CAP quotas, beyond which the production of milk would incur a levy, limited the further expansion of dairy produce. Meanwhile milk yield per cow increased appreciably, so that dairy cow numbers fell back until the milk quota was abolished in 2015.

Although agri-food exports account for less than 10 per cent of Irish merchandise exports today, unlike most of the leading non-agricultural export products, this understates their importance in that they do not embody any significant import component. Indeed, exports now account for over 90 per cent of Irish agri-food production, up from about 50 per cent before EU membership.

The UK remained the principal export market for Irish meat exports, still accounting for about a half of the total exports to the EU at Brexit. The UK is also Ireland's largest export market for dairy products, followed by the Netherlands, China, Germany and the US. Overall, the UK's share in Ireland's agri-food exports declined from about 70–80 per cent in the late 1960s, but is still about 40 per cent today.

Value added had long been neglected in an Irish food processing sector dominated by farmer cooperatives, and this meant a heavy dependence on sales of low value-added products into the EU intervention agency in the early years. Starting in the 1960s, and encouraged by the IDA, mergers and rationalizations between co-operative creamery associations resulted in a number of sizable corporate entities with a business model focused on high value-added exports. The largest of these, Kerry Group, whose origins date back to 1972, now employs some 25,000 persons in 36 countries. Once again, it is the Americas, and not Europe, which account for the largest part of their business.

And, while they began by adding value to Irish agricultural produce, only about 15 per cent of Kerry's capital assets are now located in Ireland, indicating the degree to which their production facilities are dispersed globally.

The risks of over-leveraged expansion also touched the Irish agri-food sector. The largest of the beef processing entities, Goodman International, which had built an export business to the Middle East, collapsed in controversial circumstances during the first Iraq war of 1990 and had to be restructured using new Chapter 11-type legislation.

Industrial Policy

The four freedoms, as they were progressively defined, have had the status of constitutional law in Ireland. As a result, once free trade within Europe was adopted, trade policy was no longer a matter of domestic political debate. Poorly designed protectionism was thereby avoided. Furthermore, trade agreements and EU competition law has also increasingly helped ensure an efficient and competitive domestic market for goods and some products.

But not everything was harmonized. Ireland exploited the opportunity created by the fact that taxation of corporate profits is still primarily a national responsibility in Europe, and that has allowed Ireland to maintain a very liberal corporation tax regime, with the consequences for FDI that have been described. Despite pressure from EU member states, as discussed in Section 4, Ireland retained a low corporation profits tax. Details changed over time, but since 2003 the rate has been 12.5 per cent for most firms. The extensive double taxation agreements between Ireland and other countries allowed foreign firms with operations in both high-tax and low-tax countries to pool that income, leaving little or no additional tax to be paid when the total income was repatriated to their home countries. Besides, with the US tax code in effect during most of the period under review, foreign earnings were not subject to US tax until repatriated.

If Ireland had not used the tax tool, but continued to use cultural and diasporic links to attract the US MNCs, the sectoral mix and scale of the inward investment would have been different and the scale smaller. To what extent indigenous enterprise would have made up the gap is hard to assess. A serendipitous aspect of the tax-centric policy towards MNCs was the fact that the science and technology–based sectors which could best lever the tax regime by locating profits in their Irish affiliates also proved to be rapidly growing over the entire period. Furthermore, thanks to changes in tax regimes abroad – and despite the low *rate* of tax – the revenue generated in Ireland by the tax shifting behaviour of these companies eventually became a money-spinner for the Irish government on a wholly unforeseen scale.

The much vaunted case-by-case approach to grant aid by the industrial development agencies for new capital investment was an important bargaining chip for attracting foreign investors in the early years, especially those for whom the tax arrangements were less relevant (Buckley and Ruane 2006). Competitive grant-aid from development agencies in UK regions (including Northern Ireland), for example, saw Ireland losing a number of high-profile projects during the 1980s, even though, unemployment in Ireland being very high at the time, the IDA was offering grant levels equivalent to several years of wage costs in some of the proposed projects.

State aid came increasingly under European scrutiny, especially following the creation of the Single Market (launched in 1993). Although this did not completely eliminate Irish grant-aid to industry, it had the effect of opening many markets previously dominated by government-owned or -assisted firms in other member states to competition, notably in transport, energy and communications, and it largely eliminated competition between countries in providing grant aid to business.

At home too, the trend was away from government control of firms. Not all of the privatizations that occurred can be considered successful – in some cases the new owners starved the firms they acquired of needed capital investment and overburdened them with debt (the former State-owned telephone monopoly now called Eir being a conspicuous example).

Direction of Trade

The opening up of the Irish productive sector to free trade with the bulk of the European continent did not result in an economy dominated by firms headquartered in Continental Europe. Nor has trade in goods and services concentrated there.

The headline numbers on trade show that the UK, the US and other non-EU countries now account for about two-thirds of Ireland's exports. Thus, in 2021, the EU27 accounted for only about 37 per cent of Ireland's merchandise exports, while the UK still accounted for about 11 per cent and the US for 32 per cent (Figure 4). In services, the three ratios (in 2020) were EU27=31%, UK=52% and US=14%. If the associated material, service and transfer pricing elements were netted out in order to get a picture of the geographical destination of Irish added value in exports, the EU share would be a little higher.

An even smaller share of imports is sourced from the EU: 33 per cent (merchandise) and 12 per cent (services), though it should be borne in mind that the services data is dominated by research and development services provided to MNCs from their affiliates in offshore centres.

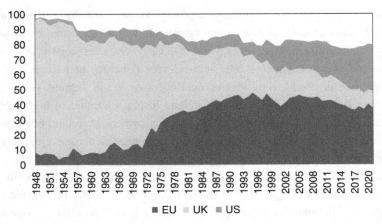

Figure 4 Main export destinations (%)

Source: IMF Direction of Trade Statistics.

The structure of the internationally trading part of the Irish business sector in the 2020s is thus dramatically different from what it was sixty years before. But the features that are so conspicuous today – the dominance of US and other MNCs, the emphasis on pharmaceuticals and the various strands of the information and information technology sector, the relatively high reported profitability – were already present within a decade of EU membership. Later years saw pharmaceuticals remaining as a leading sector, with IT manufacturing being progressively substituted by 'knowledge-based' IT services and real estate emerging (after the GFC) as a new sector of importance in FDI (Barry and Bergin 2019; Brazys and Regan 2021; Ruane et al. 2014).

All in all, the result of five decades of structural change in the Irish tradable sector has reduced its short-term price sensitivity, especially vis-à-vis the UK. Many of the sectors into which Ireland has diversified have high income elasticities of demand and, as such, a promising future. But in the longer term, Ireland's wage and price competitiveness will remain important for retaining what can be footloose industries subject to constant technological renewal.

A country is composed of people, not of firms. Section 3 turns to the people of Ireland and how they have fared in response to the changing economic conditions.

3 The Changing Population and Its Living Standards

Long before it was defined as one of the four freedoms of the EU, the relevance of freedom of movement for people can hardly be overstated for Ireland, as this de facto freedom has decisively shaped the evolution of Irish society for centuries.

Fluctuating migration flows have continued to influence the size and composition of population of Ireland in the decades of EU membership, and have done so in significantly new ways. More of the Irish-born who emigrated in their early adulthood have increasingly tended to return later, and the EU dimension became important in the past two decades as the return flows were augmented by sizable immigration especially from Eastern Europe.

A greater emphasis on educational attainment (partly funded by resources from the EU) and EU-inspired moves in the direction of greater gender equality in the workplace have helped enhance average labour productivity and contributed to increased female labour market participation.

The growing numbers at work outside of agriculture has also meant higher average living standards in the population as a whole. Helped also by a falling age-dependency during the 1990s and the early years of the 2000s, average living standards in Ireland caught up with the EU15 average and, on some metrics, exceed that average today.

While (as in many other countries in the EU and elsewhere) the market income share of top earners has increased, progressivity in the tax and social welfare system in Ireland has meant that inequality in the distribution of disposable income has tended to decline somewhat over the past couple of decades. Prosperity remains out of reach for many, though: poverty and deprivation are far from eliminated.

Freedom of Movement Predates EU Membership

The ability to emigrate has been seized over the years by millions of Irish people who, from choice or necessity, sought opportunities in destinations such as Britain, the United States, Canada and Australia. Migration flows have strongly coloured the nature of Irish society and its relations with the rest of the world, especially the English-speaking parts. The personal connections with continental European countries, through politics, culture and, in many cases religion, have also been historically strong, even though migration to these destinations has not been as large.

The flow of migration has not been all one way; even in the nineteenth century a non-negligible share of those who emigrated did return. But by 1961 the population of the Republic, at 2.8 million, was well under half of what it had been before the Great Famine in the 1840s. After 1961, each successive census showed an appreciable growth in population, something that had not been seen in Irish censuses for more than a century (Figure 5). By 2022, the population was over 5 million or just over 1 per cent of that of the EU today – much the same as it was in the much smaller 1973 Community of just nine members.

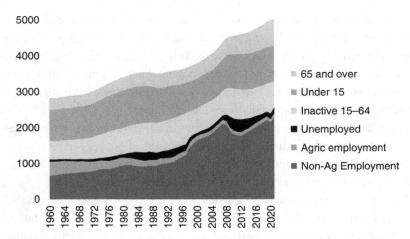

Figure 5 Population by age and employment status 1960–2021 (Thousands)
Source: Central Statistics Office. Note the strong rise in the share of the population of ages 15–64 at work, especially 1993–2007.

Since the mid-1990s the numbers returning have been swollen by immigration from new sources. The share of foreign-born people in the Irish population is now towards the high end of the European experience, even as the share of Irish-born people living abroad is also among the highest in the world.

Income and job opportunities have been the key drivers of migration flows. Rigid controls on immigration into the North American labour market were introduced in the 1920s, but, with the exception of the Second World War, and despite Brexit, there has always been free movement of labour between Ireland and Britain.[8] The UK continues to be quantitatively the principal destination for Irish emigrants.

As shown in Figure 6, there was a high rate of net emigration from Ireland from the 1920s through to 1970, as young Irish people sought better living conditions abroad. Emigration was particularly high in the 1950s, to the point where, for every three people living in Ireland in 1961, there was one Irish-born person living in Britain.

The scale of migration flows across the Irish Sea has meant that Ireland has long been part of what is effectively a common labour market with Britain, reflected in substantial two-way movements of workers, with Britain taking up the slack in Irish employment conditions. Although the overhang of under-employed agricultural workers and the generally inferior labour market

---

[8] Between 1947 and 1976 there were, however, restrictions on people moving from elsewhere in Great Britain or Ireland to work in Northern Ireland. As a result of EU entry this restriction had to be removed.

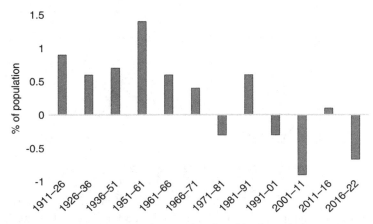

Figure 6 Ireland: Intercensal net emigration, % of population per annum
1911–2022

Source: Central Statistics Office.

conditions in Ireland resulted in a persistently higher unemployment rate than in the UK into the 1990s, fluctuations in these rates moved quite closely together. Migration flows were clearly a key equilibrating factor (Honohan 1992; Walsh 1974). And the importance of the labour market links across the Irish Sea has continued, even though the average gap between the unemployment rates in the two countries has shrunk.

The role of the EU here has been less prominent. For example, distinctive though Ireland's experience in the global financial crisis was (discussed in Section 5), it is striking to note that the timing of the fluctuations in Irish unemployment remained closely in line with that of movements in the UK, exhibiting a much closer correlation than with the euro area or with the EU as a whole – though the amplitude of the fluctuations was greater (Figure 7). The correlation with the UK seems no lower now than it was in the 1960s, showing yet again the importance of the UK economy in influencing the Irish labour market.

While average Irish wage rates in industry from the 1930s through to the early 1960s had been significantly lower than in the UK, there was a rapid catch-up in the late 1960s and early 1970s (FitzGerald 2022b). Furthermore, it is estimated that, by the early 1970s, the average purchasing power of wages was higher in Ireland. With unemployment high in the UK, this contributed to a reversal of the traditional flow of emigrants to the UK. Instead of net emigra-tion, there was a significant return flow of migrants by those who had left in the 1950s and early 1960s, as well as some immigration from Northern Ireland, driven by the outbreak there of civil unrest.

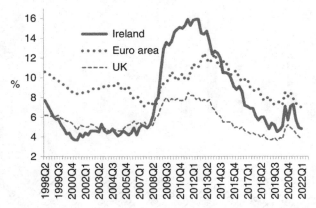

Figure 7 Unemployment rates, Ireland, UK and Euro area 1998–2022

Source: Central Statistics Office, Eurostat and Office of National Statistics, UK.

The contraction of job opportunities in Ireland associated with the recession of the 1980s (discussed in Section 5) saw a return to net emigration to the UK, even though these were years of high unemployment in Britain.

However, beginning in the mid-1990s, the combination of a vigorous economic recovery and a related rapid growth in employment opportunities saw a change in migration patterns. Many of those who had emigrated in the late 1980s returned, proving to be 'homing pigeons' rather than permanent emigrants.

Migration to and from EU and Other Countries

Up to the 1990s there was relatively limited movement of workers between Ireland and the wider EU, despite Ireland immediately establishing freedom of movement with each new wave of members. Soon, though, an increasing number of foreign-born workers also began to take up employment in Ireland. They came from other EU countries, prospective EU member states and some from further afield, including North America and Australasia. By 2002, as well as net immigration from the UK, there had been very substantial immigration from third countries (Figure 8).

While in the past many of the Irish who emigrated had had limited education, since the 1980s the bulk of Irish-born emigrants had a high level of education (Fahey et al. 1998).[9] This proved also to be the case for the foreigners moving to Ireland. Barrett et al. (2002) argue that, by expanding the pool of skilled labour,

---

[9] In 2011, 56 per cent of the Irish-born population of England and Wales had a third-level education, compared to 41 per cent in Ireland. For those aged 65 and over, though, the percentages were much lower (11 and 13 per cent respectively).

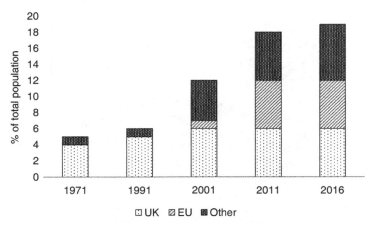

Figure 8 Place of birth of non-Irish born persons in Ireland on census day
1971–2016

Source: Central Statistics Office.

Note: In the figure 'EU' refers to countries who were member states in the relevant year
so that, for example, for 2002 the candidate countries that joined in May 2004 are
excluded, but they are included for 2011.

this influx of skilled foreigners helped the economy to grow more rapidly. In
turn, the more rapid growth attracted a significant number of Irish nationals with
lower levels of education into the labour market.

The most significant opening of the Irish labour to new member states
occurred in 2004, with the enlargement including eight CEE countries, and it
led to a huge inflow of young adults joining the Irish labour market.[10] This
enabled large-scale immigration from Central and Eastern European (CEE)
member states (Figure 8). The very rapid economic growth of the period
2000 to 2007 was facilitated by this influx of new workers, especially into
the construction sector. While the financial crisis from 2008 saw many of
these recent arrivals return to their home countries, especially construction
workers, nonetheless they still accounted for 6 per cent of the population in
2011.

Of the foreign nationals counted in the 2011 Irish Census of Population,
almost a quarter were born in Poland and 42 per cent in the ten CEE member
states. At that time UK nationals accounted for over 20 per cent, and the rest of
the EU for fewer than 9 per cent. More than 70 per cent of foreign nationals in
Ireland at that date were from the EU (including the UK) (Figure 9).

---

[10] Only Sweden and the UK joined Ireland in this immediate opening up.

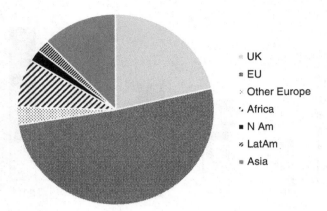

Figure 9 Ireland: Foreign nationals by region of birth 2011
Source: Central Statistics Office.

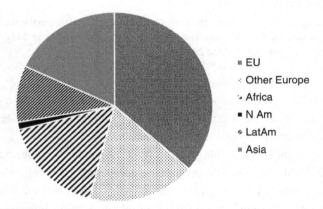

Figure 10 EU: Foreign-born population by region of birth 2011
Source: Eurostat.

Although not measuring the same concept as nationality, it is interesting to note that, elsewhere in Europe, far more of the foreign-born residents came from outside the EU than from other EU countries (Figure 10).

Still, the inflow to Ireland was not just from Europe: Asia accounted for 12 per cent, Africa for 8 per cent and the Americas for almost 5 per cent.

The influx of returning Irish emigrants and new arrivals from other countries resulted in a rapid growth in the Irish population in the 2000s. Many of the newcomers were well educated and in relatively highly paid employment; they also sought good accommodation. These inflows contributed to the upward pressure on the cost of housing associated with the property bubble of those years

(Duffy et al. 2005). Housing costs were beginning to limit the attractiveness of Ireland to those coming from elsewhere in the EU before the financial collapse of 2008.

The financial crisis saw a temporary return to net emigration after 2008, as many foreign workers who lost their jobs went back to their home countries and many young Irish sought employment elsewhere in countries less affected by the economic downturn. However, with the economic recovery there has been a return to significant net immigration since 2015, which continued even through the pandemic. This time many of the new arrivals are coming from outside the EU, as the gap in real wage rates between Ireland and countries such as Poland and Latvia has narrowed considerably since they joined the EU. Also, large numbers of refugees arrived from Ukraine in 2022. Despite the sharp fall in housing prices in the financial crisis, the cost of housing has returned as a substantial discouragement to immigration in recent years.

Outward flows from Ireland to EU countries other than the UK have been more muted. Relatively few Irish people have taken advantage of freedom of movement to settle elsewhere in the EU, so Ireland is rather lightly represented among the foreign-born population in other member states. In 2011, just over 1 per cent of Irish-born people lived in EU countries apart from the UK. Of course, the situation with the UK is different: more than one in six of UK residents born elsewhere in the EU in 2011 came from Ireland.

Temporary emigration by young Irish people to seek employment abroad has been a constant feature of the Irish labour market. This emigration occurs even when the economy is growing rapidly, as young people seek new experiences and adventure abroad. At each census over the past three decades, between 15 and 20 per cent of those aged between 40 and 65 have been returned emigrants. It has long been a feature of this return migration that those with a third-level education are more likely to return. The proportion of people with a third-level education who are returned emigrants is much higher than for the rest of the population.

Whereas the earlier period of substantial net emigration narrowed the horizon of those who stayed at home, the more recent period of higher return migration and immigration, much of it from the newer EU member states, has enriched Irish society in many diverse and incalculable ways.

The pattern of return migration is important to the economy, facilitating more rapid growth. Barrett and Goggin (2010) found a wage premium of 7 per cent for returning men and women who had worked abroad. The premium was also higher for people with post-graduate degrees and those who worked outside Europe. This higher level of remuneration reflects higher productivity in the workplace.

Having such a high proportion of the population who had gained experience abroad has contributed significantly to the opening up of the Irish economy as well as to the rapid growth of productivity since 1990. While much of the management of foreign MNCs operating in Ireland in the 1970s was by foreigners, today most of the managers are Irish people who have returned from working for multinationals in foreign labour markets. They have developed the requisite management skills on the job across the globe.

Demographic Structure

As well as the impact of continuing large migration flows, the structure of the Irish population has also been affected by differences in fertility compared to many other EU countries. In 1960 the Total Fertility Rate (TFR) in Ireland was 3.8, much higher than the 2.7 or so reported for countries such as Denmark, France and the UK. By 1973, when Ireland joined the EU, the TFR in Ireland was still 3.7 compared to around 2 for most other EU countries. Thereafter, Irish fertility fell more rapidly, eventually converging on EU rates of between 1.8 and 2.0 in 1990. Today the TFR in Ireland is 1.6 – very similar to the rate of 1.5 for the EU as a whole. The Irish population has thus joined the rest of the EU in not replacing itself.

The delayed fall in fertility compared to its EU neighbours meant that the natural increase in the population was much higher in Ireland up to the late 1990s. Because of the high birth rate and the emigration of the 1950s to the UK, the economic dependency rate in Ireland (the ratio of the non-working population to those at work) has followed a very different trajectory from much of the rest of the EU.

In 1973, each person in paid employment was supporting 1.7 persons who were not in employment, either through their pay packet or through the taxes that they paid. This dependency ratio rose to two people not working for every person in paid employment in the mid-1980s, adding to the economic burdens of that time.

However, a combination of the fall in youth dependency (as the birth rate fell) and the fact that many of those who had been born in Ireland in the 1940s and were now elderly had emigrated in their youth reduced the economic dependency rate in Ireland to one person supported by each person in paid employment in the mid-2000s. This easing in the dependency ratio contributed to the growing prosperity in Ireland in those boom years, and was not mirrored in most other EU countries.

But this favourable trend has come to an end as the population living in Ireland ages. Ireland has joined most other EU countries in seeing, once more, an increase in the dependency ratio, and this can be expected to rise steadily. Nevertheless, at present the ratio, at about 1, is still well below the EU average of 1.3. Indeed, old-age dependency is lower in Ireland than in any other member state (apart from Luxembourg) and will continue to be so over the coming decade.

Education

In the immediate post-war years most countries in Northern Europe, from the Soviet Union through to the UK, invested in upgrading their educational systems. Ireland was an exception in this regard, following instead a pattern observed in southern Europe, where there was limited access to second-level education. Ireland was slow to follow the UK, which introduced free second-level education in its 1944 Education Act. In Ireland, until 1967 secondary education was reserved for those who could afford to pay for it. As a result, for the cohort of children born between 1951 and 1955, only 50 per cent completed high school while only 20 per cent ended up with a third-level qualification (Figure 11a). This pattern was similar to that observed in Spain, Italy and Greece. By contrast, for children in countries such as Finland, Poland, Germany, the US and Estonia (then part of the Soviet Union) at least three quarters completed upper secondary education.

By the 1960s, Ireland's laggard status in regard to education had become apparent to national specialists who mobilized the support of the OECD, leading to an influential report, published in 1965, which highlighted Ireland's poor education and the likely impact this was having on national economic performance compared to its Northern European neighbours (Department of Education 1965). The OECD report's key recommendation, that upper secondary education should be provided free of charge for all, was implemented in 1967. In the decades that followed, there was further extensive investment in education at both second and third levels.

As a result of these education policy initiatives, for the cohort of children born between 1981 and 1985 – the first to benefit fully from the 1967 reforms – education attainment was very different from that for their parents born thirty years earlier (Figure 11b). For this cohort Ireland joined the countries with the highest completion rates for upper secondary education such as the US, Poland, Finland and Germany. Under 15 per cent of the cohort left school with only lower secondary education; Ireland also had one of the highest proportions of young people completing third-level education at over 40 per cent, in line with the top countries. The OECD Programme for International Student Assessment (PISA) shows Irish second-level students consistently performing above the OECD average in reading, mathematics and science.

While the impact of this change in educational policy drew on the wider European experience, it was not directly driven by EU legislation, as education remains a largely national responsibility.

Without attempting to delve deeply here into the quality and effectiveness of the educational provision, it is clear that there have been European influences. Alongside the well-trodden path of Irish undergraduate students to work in summer

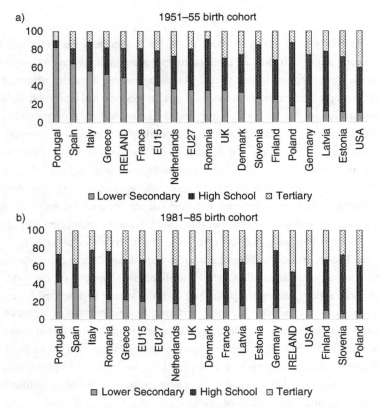

Figure 11 Educational attainment in EU countries of persons born in
(a) 1951–5; (b) 1981–5

Source: Eurostat.

service jobs in the United States came the Erasmus programme, where many students at Irish third-level institutions were facilitated in spending a period in a university elsewhere in Europe, adding to their experience.

The increased public spending on education was partly covered by sums received from the EU Structural Funds (discussed in Section 4). Approximately 30 per cent of these EU transfers went to support training, as well as some limited investment in education that was permitted under the scheme's rules.

The rising educational attainment of the labour force significantly influenced the growth of the economy through three different channels: by making people more employable, through raising the participation rate, especially for women, and through raising productivity (FitzGerald 2012a).

In the wider EU labour market, the demand for workers with third-level qualifications has risen continuously over the last twenty-five years, while the demand for those with only a lower secondary education has fallen. By better matching the skills of the labour force to the demands of the labour market, the probability of workers experiencing unemployment is substantially reduced.

Back in 1990, 80 per cent of the large number of unemployed had not completed their secondary education, which made their chances of finding a job in the subsequent recovery much more difficult. By contrast, after the financial crisis, while the unemployment rate again peaked at over 15 per cent in 2012, just six years later it had fallen below 6 per cent. This partly reflected the fact that 70 per cent of the unemployed in 2012 had at least upper secondary education.

Although Irish women have traditionally been more likely to have at least an upper secondary education than men, their participation in the Irish labour force was low by EU standards in the early 1970s. Until EU entry in 1973, women also suffered from significant legal disadvantages in the labour market. In the public service women had to resign on marriage and married men were paid more than women or single men. Because of the EU requirement that women be treated equally in the labour market, these restrictions were rapidly removed after EU entry. Nonetheless, these discriminatory measures, combined with the cultural background which they reflected, helped keep female labour force participation levels well below those in other EU members in the 1970s and 1980s.

Another factor discouraging female labour force participation was the fact that the progressive personal income tax was applied to the joint income of married couples. Differences across Europe in this dimension are correlated with differences in female labour force participation, with women in joint-assessment systems (like that in Ireland and Germany) being less likely to join the labour force than those in individual-assessment countries in Scandinavia (Fuchs-Schundeln 2019). This reflects the high marginal tax rate facing the lower earning partner, often a woman, as they consider participating in the labour force. The net financial benefit from working is greatly reduced, especially given the high costs of child-care in Ireland.

Over time, the opening up of Irish society to the outside world, combined with the return of many emigrants who had experienced life abroad, brought a gradual cultural change that contributed to an increase in female labour force participation.

Also, reflecting the strong association between educational attainment and female participation, the wider access to secondary education and the related rapid increase in female educational attainment between 1990 and 2010 can be credited with adding about half a percentage point per annum to the growth in the labour force. Labour force participation rates for young female graduates converged on those experienced in other EU labour markets.

Finally, and most importantly, the rising educational attainment of the labour force substantially increased its productivity. Between 1986 and 1996 the rising educational attainment of the population probably contributed about one percentage point a year to economic growth through enhancing labour productivity. Averaging over the longer period from 1960 to 1992 this effect contributed around another 0.5 percentage point a year to economic growth. An even higher figure of 1.3 percentage points a year is estimated for the period between 1992 and 2010 (Durkan et al. 1999; FitzGerald 2012a).

Education also played a part in ensuring that Ireland was an attractive destination for inward foreign direct investment. Analysis of the determinants of FDI inflows across EU regions confirms the importance of the supply of graduates (Siedschlag and Koecklin 2019).

The combination of different factors, the natural increase in the population, migration and changes in labour force participation have contributed to a rapid growth in the labour force since Ireland joined the EU in 1973. Over almost fifty years labour force growth averaged 1.6 per cent a year. During the period 1990 to 2005 the growth rate was 2.8 per cent a year. This has been an important factor in the rapid growth of the economy, especially in the period since 1990. While the growth rate of the labour force has slowed in recent years, nonetheless, it is an important factor explaining why the Irish economy continues to grow more rapidly than the rest of the EU.

Wages

In the past, developments in the UK labour market influenced developments in the Irish labour market, reflecting the free movement of workers between the two countries. While wage rates in Irish industry had been significantly lower than in the UK in the post-war years, by the time Ireland joined the EU in 1973 they had largely converged on UK rates (FitzGerald 2022b). As shown in Figure 12a, the average purchasing power of wage rates was also already close to wage rates in France in the 1970s, though well below that in Germany. Despite these wage rates, though, as elaborated below, the average standard of living in Ireland was well below the average for the EU15 until about 1990, mainly because of Ireland's relatively low share of population at work outside of agriculture.

Since the 1970s real wage rates in Ireland have followed a fairly similar path to wage rates in France and the UK, though over the past decade a small gap has opened up with UK rates. However, this may be due to changes in the relative human capital of the workforces in Ireland and the UK.

Because social insurance and other taxes on labour were much lower in Ireland than in most other EU countries (other than the UK and Denmark)

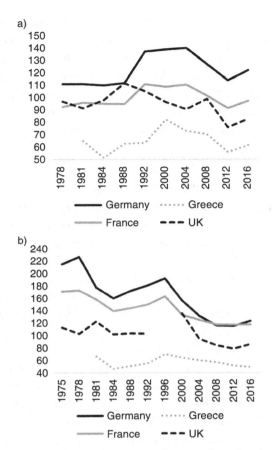

Figure 12a Average hourly wage rates in manufacturing (adjusted for purchasing power), selected EU countries, relative to Ireland=100

Source: Authors' calculations based on Eurostat.

Figure 12b Average hourly labour costs in manufacturing, selected EU countries, relative to Ireland=100

Source: Authors' calculations based on Eurostat.

labour costs for employers were significantly lower than in most other member states when Ireland joined the EU in 1973. Thus, in terms of labour cost competitiveness, Ireland was an attractive location for inward investment for businesses aiming to supply the EU market. However, as shown in Figure 12b, this competitiveness advantage has been eroded over time, reflecting the wider convergence in living standards in Ireland to the levels of the most prosperous members of the EU.

The growth of foreign MNCs in Ireland has also affected wage rates. Those working in foreign MNCs have traditionally been paid significantly more than in Irish-owned firms. In 2018 average earnings in foreign MNCs were over €62,000, whereas in Irish-owned MNCs they were €54,000 and in all other Irish-owned companies they were €37,000. These differences partly reflected differences in the sectors in which they operated and in the human capital of the work force, with foreign MNCs employing more graduates.

Average Living Standards

The sharp rise in per capita GNI and GDP in Ireland over the past three decades should not be taken as an indication of the development in average living standards, given the large distortions (already mentioned above) introduced into the national accounts by the transactions of multinational corporations (FitzGerald 2022a; Honohan 2021). Nevertheless, that there has been a strong increase in average living standards in Ireland both absolutely and relative to other member states is confirmed by other indicators. Two of these are shown in Figure 13. One is the Ireland-specific concept modified gross national income (GNI*), developed (as mentioned above) as an attempt to exclude the main distortions from the MNC sector in order to make it more internationally comparable to GNI. The other concept, 'actual individual consumption' (of households and of government on behalf of households), is a standard international concept which is free of the distortions from MNCs, but excludes national savings which can impact the future standard of living. Broadly speaking, the main fluctuations in both series and their overall trend are similar, though there has been a divergence in the most recent years.

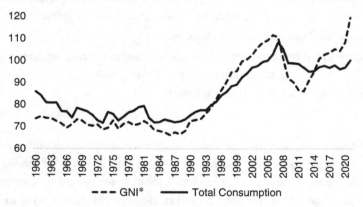

Figure 13 Per capita modified gross national income (GNI*) and consumption (adjusted for purchasing power) as % EU15 average

Source: Authors' calculations based on Central Statistics Office and Eurostat.

In the (modified) income comparison of average living standards, Ireland languished at about 70 per cent of the EU15 average from 1960 till the early 1990s; but then Ireland's per capita income, rose rapidly to 110 per cent of the EU15 average before the financial crisis. There was then a sharp fall, followed by a strong recovery after 2013 and a jump in 2021 to a new peak of 120 per cent of the EU15 average which, on this data, brings Ireland into the leading group of EU countries for that year – trailing only about four others.

The per capita consumption indicator places Ireland at about 80 per cent of the EU15 average between 1960 and 1980. The impact of the fiscal crisis saw this measure fall to near 70 per cent of the EU15 average in the 1980s as a result of the major fiscal tightening, before a rapid convergence began in the early 1990s continuing in the pre-GFC years to reach a peak of 108 per cent of the EU15 average. Although the subsequent dip was less than that affecting income, the consumption measure of living standards has not yet recovered its 2007 peak and stands today at the EU15 average.

In order to understand the divergence between the two measures in the last few years, it is necessary to recall the standard national income identity in which national savings (private plus government) equals investment plus the current account of the balance of payments. The major difference between the national income and consumption is thus national savings (or equivalently investment plus the balance of payments). The jump in the GNI* series in 2021 is strongly influenced by the huge corporation tax receipts in that year, which allowed the Government to avoid substantial dissaving, even as it increased spending during the pandemic and as household savings jumped. This suggests that at least some of the gap that opened up between the two measures is likely to be temporary, and to be reversed when tax receipts normalize.

Inequality and Social Welfare

How the benefits of economic growth are distributed across the population has in recent times at last begun to receive the attention it deserves, partly driven by a growing awareness of the extent to which the fruits of US economic growth have accrued to the highest-income groups. Europe's experience has been less extreme, and Ireland has tracked more closely the average of EU experience in this respect than the US. It has also diverged from the experience in the UK, especially during the 1980s.

Inequality of income and wealth is influenced by both national economic performance and policy. Low inequality requires maintenance of high employment as well as access to education. It can also be strongly influenced by the structure and extent of taxation and social protection. These are largely national responsibilities.

In the period before Ireland joined the EU it had a more limited welfare system than its continental European neighbours. While this was largely a matter for national policy, the greater exposure of policymakers to the experience of other EU countries helped bring greater focus to this deficit in Irish social policy. Although major structural elements of the Irish social welfare system stayed within the model adapted from the UK, the 1970s duly saw a significant expansion in the coverage of the welfare system with the introduction of new schemes. Indeed, despite the difficult economic conditions, Irish welfare payment rates were increased more rapidly in the 1980s than in the UK. The upward trend in the real value of social welfare payments continued up to the onset of the 2008 recession.

There are many dimensions to inequality. Here we confine attention to measures of aggregate income inequality across households. The growth over the past 50 years in the pre-tax income share of the top 10 per cent – one convenient measure of inequality – shows Ireland close to the middle ground, with a lower increase than in the UK or Germany, for example, but higher than in France or Italy (Figure 14). The increase is much smaller than that in the United States.

The Gini coefficient, which draws on data across all income levels, provides an alternative lens on inequality. Estimates of the Gini from sample surveys – admittedly subject to sizable sampling error – suggest that, after an improvement in some earlier years, the boom of the early 2000s saw a widening in the dispersion of market incomes in Ireland (though administered minimum wage rates provided some insulation, as noted by Holton and O'Neill 2017). However, this trend has since been reversed.

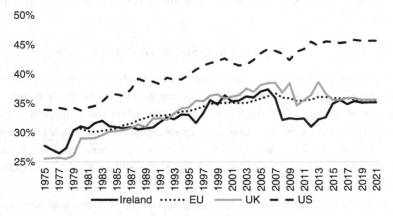

Figure 14 Income share (pre-tax) of the top 10% (of tax units), Ireland, EU, UK, US, 1975–2021

Source: World Inequality Database.

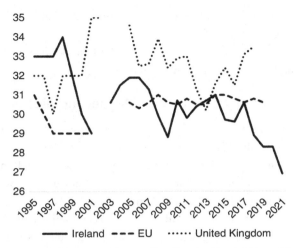

Figure 15 Gini coefficient of inequality (equivalized disposable income), Ireland, EU, UK. 1995–2021

Source: Eurostat, Central Statistics Office.

Note: Roantree et al. (2021) suggest somewhat lower numbers for Ireland in the 1990s.

The income tax and social welfare system has been a key contributor to limiting the inequality of disposable income. In general, survey data show the substantial impact of the social welfare system, and especially the tax system, on inequality in disposable income (Voitchovsky et al. 2012). Sample survey estimates of the Gini index for equivalized disposable income put Ireland close to the median of EU countries and point to a decline in inequality on this measure relative to that in the EU and the UK (Figure 15). Several other analyses of the data on disposable income confirm that Ireland's economic and public policy performance through both boom and bust appears to have been in the direction of a reduction in inequality – though it should not be forgotten that any given percentage fall in incomes will surely have hit the poor hardest (e.g. Madden 2014; Nolan and Maître 2000; Roantree et al. 2021).

Other inequalities persist, for example across generations, where the rising cost of housing has adversely impacted the prosperity of younger cohorts.

Much of social policy is a matter for national governments more than for the EU. Nevertheless, through channels such as peer review of national policies on poverty and social exclusion, European social policy is generally thought to have had a notable impact on Irish social policy over the years. This has been clearest in the field of gender equality, but also more widely moving away from what analysts describe as a patriarchal and familial orientation, though remaining focused on poverty reduction rather than equality. Europe has also given a voice and a forum to Irish social policy activists who, in turn, have had some influence in the evolution of EU anti-poverty and exclusion programmes (Murphy 2015; Ó Cinnéide 2010).

As well as the direct impact of EU law on Ireland, this kind of indirect impact on ideas and attitudes is taken up in Section 4.

4 Institutional Change and Microeconomic Policy

Mid-century Ireland was not only a closed economy, but in many respects a closed society (Daly 2016; Garvin 2005; Lee 1989). Few emigrants were returning to infuse new thinking from their broader experience. Public administration and other economic institutions, such as the trade union movement, had operated largely according to the models inherited from Britain.

Since then, Europe has strongly influenced Irish economic institutions. While some changes came through EU legislation, at least as important has been the fact that EU membership exposed Ireland more directly to a diversity of ideas as it increased its engagement with a multilateral and multicultural socio-economic space. The membership decision in 1973 was broadly welcomed, and attitudes to the EU have remained positive.

In particular, EU membership changed the management of Ireland's external official economic relations, opening new opportunities for international coalition formation. Financial assistance from Europe also catalysed improvements in the efficiency of the Irish administrative system. Evolving EU microeconomic policies focused Irish government policies, though often less thoroughly than envisaged by Europe.

Initially, the Common Agricultural Policy (CAP) provided major support for the farming sector, which had previously relied on significant domestic subsidies. In the late 1980s and the early 1990s the development of the EU's Structural Fund support for less developed regions also proved important. These transfers came at an important turning point, encouraging investment in key areas of infrastructure. Furthermore, the process of absorbing the EU Structural Funds not only boosted national income directly, but also strengthened the governance and planning of multi-year public spending.

Like trade policy, EU microeconomic policies in fields such as competition, energy and the environment have had an effect in stiffening Irish government measures that protect the common good in the face of sectoral interests. Of course not all of these policies were ideally adapted to Ireland's needs or preferences: growing pressure to harmonize corporation tax regimes across the EU is a recent case in point.

Northern Ireland's experience provides a counterpoint. Although, as part of the UK, it too joined in 1973, and although it too benefitted from CAP subsidies and Structural Funds, the relationship was largely mediated through London. Governmental and economic institutions in Northern Ireland were not comparably transformed by new continental connections.

Attitudes to the EU

In the 1972 referendum on EU membership, 83 per cent of the population voted in favour. This was not just because of the evident benefit to farmers from higher food prices, trumpeted by advocates of membership. After all, farmers accounted for only a quarter of those employed, and the whole population would face the higher food prices. Even more important was a consciousness that Ireland was falling behind economic advances in the rest of Europe. Also, the prospect of finally escaping economic dependence on the UK held many attractions for those who saw it as a final step in establishing Irish economic independence, half a century after political independence had been achieved.

Although the diverse factors affecting the well-being of individuals and households in Ireland clearly extend well beyond the direct remit of the EU, today a large proportion of surveyed Irish people value Ireland's EU membership. Even in the difficult years of the euro area crisis and the programme of fiscal austerity monitored by the EU-led *Troika* (2011–13), more Irish people had a positive image of the EU than had a negative image; and the Irish positive percentage was higher than in the EU as a whole.

Of those surveyed in 2022 for Eurobarometer, more than seven in ten Irish people reported a positive view of the EU, putting Ireland close to the top of the list of member states by this measure. Indeed, for decades there has been a higher proportion of positive Irish respondents than in the EU as a whole. More than three in five Irish respondents in 2022 said that they trust the Union's chief institutions (Parliament, Commission, Council, Central Bank); and the same proportion felt that the Union was going in the right direction – far higher than the 37 per cent holding the same opinion elsewhere in the EU.

The widely held perception that EU membership has been good for Ireland has many sources, of which the stronger economic performance in the half-century of membership compared with the previous half-century is just one component. Irish people, long used to spending time working or studying abroad, or having relatives abroad, are comfortable with juggling multiple national identities. They recognize how Ireland's national sovereignty has been strengthened through participating in the larger, albeit shallower, sovereignty of the Union's polity in which the voting power of small states has been disproportionate to their population. For most it has, though, been a gradual process of recognizing benefits to Ireland of the European connection rather than a commitment to a reasoned concept of Europe.

International Economic Relations

Through membership of organizations such as the International Monetary Fund (IMF), the World Bank and the OEEC/OECD, from the late 1950s Irish policymakers had some contact with the economic world beyond the UK. But trade policy remained focused on the UK and the currency remained pegged to sterling. Ireland was in a weak position in all economic negotiations with the UK: effectively a supplicant seeking better access to the UK market with little to offer in return.

EU membership radically changed this situation. The move to multilateral negotiations within the EU institutions had a transformative effect on the Irish civil service. As the poorest member of the then nine member states, Ireland in 1973 was individually in a weak bargaining position. But its rights as a member state were enshrined in EU laws, and the diverse membership of the EU meant that shifting coalitions could be formed to further Irish economic interests over subsequent decades.

Participation of Irish civil servants and politicians in the administrative and political structures of the Union has helped develop a broader awareness in Ireland of the possible approaches to national economic policy than existed when Britain was the chief role model.

In the early years of membership the flow of subsidies from the CAP supported farm incomes and allowed a reduction in Irish Government expenditure on agriculture. The subsidies amounted to over 3 per cent of national income rising to almost 4 per cent in the 1980s. (Today they still amount to just under 1 per cent of modified national income.) Ireland was not the only country for which the CAP was important: the French Government, in particular, sought to protect and develop the CAP. From the beginning, the strongest opponent of the CAP was the UK. But France was strongly in favour, so the Irish authorities sought the protection of a French 'umbrella' in forming a coalition to protect the CAP. Immediately, this highlighted the changed international economic policy environment. In many other fields, Ireland found strong allies across the EU, including the UK, with which to pursue its economic interests.

Ireland's diplomatic priorities within the EU have evolved over time. By the late 1980s the importance of agriculture in the Irish economy was declining and, with Greece, Spain and Portugal joining, much greater attention was given to new instruments to promote economic convergence within the EU. These instruments came to be referred to as the Structural Funds, and they involved significant EU transfers to the weaker regions and member states to support additional investment. Ireland had already attracted significant help in this form in the 1980s, amounting to around 1.5 per cent of national income, but Ireland sought and got support within the EU for a large increase in Structural Funds from 1989 onwards. Germany, as the largest indirect contributor to the Structural Funds, supported Ireland's ambitions. In 1992, the second round of the process saw a major further allocation for Ireland for the period to 1999. The result was that Structural Fund transfers to Ireland amounted to almost 2.5 per cent of national income between 1990 and 1994 and to almost 2 per cent of the larger Irish national income in the period 1995–9. Thereafter, the transfers fell sharply, down to only 0.4 per cent of national income in the first decade of the new millennium, reflecting the improvement in Irish living standards.

The main focus of attention of Irish economic diplomacy within the EU gradually shifted over the 1990s to protecting the low corporation tax regime. Even though many member states have operated selective corporation tax regimes, Ireland's inducements in this respect were – and still are – viewed with some reservations in Europe. While taxation is largely a national matter, with EU law in this respect governed by unanimity, Ireland was, as already mentioned in Section 2, coming under increasing pressure on this front.[11]

The original corporation tax regime, established in 1956, exempted profits from exporting. The Anglo-Irish Free Trade Agreement of 1965 envisaged abolition of this exemption in the mid-1970s. EU membership in 1973 superseded that agreement, but this export tax relief – clearly inappropriate for the common market – was soon replaced by a 10 per cent corporation tax rate on new manufacturing; this was applied to all manufacturing firms from 1990 (later internationally traded services were added).

As this still looked like a de facto promotion of export sectors, further pressure from the EU caused the distinction between the tax on these sectors and the rest of the corporate sector to be removed, thereby almost incidentally lowering the rate on domestically oriented sectors. In 1996, a common corporate tax rate for all activity (of 12.5 per cent) was announced to apply from 2003. While the EU Commission would have preferred the common rate to be 15 per cent, domestic advocates for foreign investment, in particular the state's IDA, won the day, and the rate was set at 12.5 per cent.

To protect the position on corporation tax, successive governments worked to build support among other member states. For much of the last thirty years countries such as the UK and Sweden have had their own reasons for guarding national independence in the setting of domestic tax regimes. In 1992 the Irish

---

[11] For example, in 2010, some governments wanted to use Ireland's need for emergency financial support to leverage change in the corporate tax regime. However, this was opposed by the Commission and the IMF.

government opposed the introduction of a harmonized EU-wide carbon tax, partly because of concerns that it could lead to harmonization of other taxes.

As more and more of the leading information technology firms consolidated their presence in Ireland in the 1990s, several began to exploit complexities in the tax codes of Ireland and other countries to increase the part of their global operations that would be taxed in Ireland and/or drive the effective rate of tax on their operations well below the headline figure of 10 per cent which was in operation from 1981 (12.5 per cent from 2003). This behaviour accelerated sharply from 2015, boosting the Irish Government's tax revenues (and, as mentioned, making the GDP figures meaningless). The extreme use of these features of the tax code was strongly criticized by other member states, and by the European Commission. In respect of one particular tax interpretation, the latter asserted (in 2016) that Ireland had given the giant IT company Apple an unfair competitive advantage, and called for retrospective taxation of that company. This decision of the Commission was challenged not only by Apple but also by the Irish Government which insisted that no special advantage had been granted to Apple; that challenge was upheld by the European General Court. (This decision in turn is being appealed by the Commission.)

The international agreement brokered in 2021 by the OECD on a 15 per cent minimum corporation tax rate, with special provision for taxing profits from large IT service companies, may be about to bring closure to most of this diplomatic saga.

The original EU Single Market was significantly influenced by the then UK government, and it has subsequently proved to be very important for the Irish economy. With the UK's exit from the EU, Ireland in the coming years will have to seek support from other countries, such as those in Scandinavia and the Netherlands, to ensure the EU's continued commitment to an open globalized economy, so important for the Irish economy.

EU Structural Funds

The EU Structural Funds were particularly important for Ireland in the period 1990 to 1994, just as Ireland was emerging from a severe fiscal adjustment. Public investment, largely in infrastructure, had fallen from being over 5 per cent of national income in 1980 to 2 per cent in 1988, as the public finance crisis was tackled.

The Structural Funds enabled a resumption of public investment spending to support Ireland's future economic growth. As the EU payments were conditional on matching government funding, they provided an important motivation to raise public investment, at a time when domestic political forces had given this less priority. As the decade progressed and the economy began to grow rapidly, the EU Structural Funds process became less influential. By the end of the 1990s the Irish Government would likely have financed the public investment itself, even without the EU transfers.

In its approach to the allocation of the transfers to different types of investment Ireland showed rather different priorities than the other three 'cohesion' countries: Greece, Portugal and Spain. Ireland chose to invest more in human capital (education and training) and less in physical infrastructure than, for example, Portugal (FitzGerald 2006). This reflected the available research, which suggested a higher return to this form of investment (FitzGerald et al. 1999; Honohan 1997).

The direct impact of the additional investment, funded by EU transfers, on the growth of the economy in the middle years of the 1990s, was significant but not transformative. FitzGerald (1998) and Bradley et al. (2003) estimated a cumulative long-term impact of the Structural Funds transfers of the 1990s on the level of national income of around 3 per cent. This reflected the expanded supply capacity of the economy once the investment had taken place. The short-term impact was significantly higher, because of the effects on aggregate demand of the additional investment. While important, this accounts for only a limited share of the exceptional growth of those Celtic Tiger years.

Probably more important than the EU transfers themselves was the institutional change which was associated with the investment process. The transfers were made on condition that each country develop a multi-year investment plan. The plan needed to be supported by ex ante evidence on the likely beneficial impact of individual investments (cf. Casey 2022).[12]

This brought about a number of institutional changes in Ireland, which were of lasting benefit. During the fiscal crisis years of the 1980s long-term planning of investment had effectively been suspended: the financial constraints of those years resulted in uncoordinated decision-making from one year to the next. A road project might be begun but completion could be delayed for many years, depending on financial constraints. In contrast, from 1990 onwards, successive national plans set out medium-term investment programmes, and these were largely implemented.

An elaborate evaluation process was established in the 1990s. Before each national plan was finalized, independent research was undertaken to establish priorities and, at the mid-stage in each plan, a new evaluation was undertaken to provide a basis for reprioritization.

---

[12] Regional policy within Ireland intersected tangentially with the EU Structural Funds with the identification of a Border Midlands and Western Region (BMW) in order to optimize on access to some of the Funds to which the economy as a unit would not have been eligible.

The success in implementing this evidence-based approach to policy formation in the first planning period from 1989 to 1992 led to Ireland receiving an additional allocation of funds which had become available because they could not be absorbed by other countries. Good governance was rewarded.

While this process worked well in the 1990s, as the size of the EU transfers dropped after 2000 so too did EU leverage in terms of Irish decision-making. From the early 2000s, less and less attention was given to developing the evidence base for decision-making on investment (FitzGerald 2012b). In addition, repeated warnings that the public investment ambition, now largely funded by Irish taxes, was unduly stimulatory were ignored (Barrett et al. 2007; FitzGerald et al. 2003).

While this departure from the established institutional procedures of the 1990s contributed to unwise decision-making in the run-up to the financial crisis, over the last decade there has been a return to the more structured approach to prioritizing public investment.

In particular the establishment of the Government's Economic Service after the financial crisis reflected acceptance that a good evidence base was essential in prioritizing public investment. This return to the governance of the 1990s can be seen as a lasting legacy of the EU Structural Funds process.

The EU Commission and the ECB were also involved (along with the IMF) in negotiating and supervising the policy conditions under which the programme of financial assistance to Ireland was granted in 2010 during the financial crisis. The creation of an Irish Fiscal Advisory Council in 2011 was part of the package of policies agreed, and represented another institutional strengthening, in this case inspired by an emerging EU consensus. Public management reform per se was not part of the programme conditionality, but the severe reductions in government expenditure required under the programme legitimated implementation of a set of reforms to what had, according to an OECD report, become a 'fragmented, complex and increasingly expensive administrative apparatus' (MacCarthaigh and Hardiman 2020). Once again, by providing an external reference point, Europe helped stiffen Irish administrative governance arrangements, albeit indirectly.

EU Budget

Compared with national governments, the budget of the EU, funded by national contributions broadly proportionate to GDP, is a much smaller percentage of EU GDP, still closer to 1 per cent than 2 per cent. Nevertheless, through both the funding of the CAP, and later through the Structural and Cohesion Funds,

Ireland has been a substantial net beneficiary of grant assistance from the EU budget, especially in the 1990s.

The Irish gross contribution to the EU budget has averaged a little over 1 per cent of national income since the early 1980s, and until very recently Ireland was a net beneficiary through EU transfers. This reflected the fact that the CAP-related subsidies are very substantial, and for four decades this more than offset Ireland's budgetary contribution.

While Ireland was a net beneficiary from the EU budget, Irish governments favoured expanding it. Even now that Ireland has become a net contributor, Irish Government policy still favours a larger EU budget. This partly reflects a determination that solidarity with poorer member states is important, but it also reflects the fact that a larger budget relieves pressures on the CAP, which remains important to Irish farming.

Because the budgetary contribution is related to GNI, which for Ireland is, as mentioned, boosted by the accounting treatment of MNCs, it could be argued that Ireland's budgetary contribution is unduly high. If it were related instead to the modified gross national income GNI*, which excludes such distortions, the contribution would be reduced by over 25 per cent. However, this argument has not been made by Irish governments, considering that the €15 billion in exceptional corporation tax revenue that accrued to Ireland from the profits of the MNCs in 2021 is about ten times as large.

Economic Culture

When Ireland became independent it adopted the governmental institutions inherited from British rule with only limited changes. For example, to help establish an Irish Department of Finance in 1922 the UK Treasury 'lent' a number of its staff to Ireland. This brought essential technical experience, and it also helped reinforce the adoption of UK ways of managing the public administration and the wider economy. For many years, British administrative practice continued to influence developments in Ireland (Fanning 1978).

The need to maintain access to the UK market meant that in the post-war years there was continuing frequent and generally collaborative interaction between UK and Irish civil servants dealing with economic policy. In the 1960s the Department of Finance relied for external economic advice on a number of UK academic economists. Thus even after fifty years of independence the institutions of government in Ireland and the UK were still closely related, with very limited influence on the Irish administration from developments in other European countries.

All this changed at the beginning of 1973. The files on Ireland's external economic relations, predominantly with the UK, were archived and new files dealing with the wide range of EU institutions and committees were opened. From the beginning, civil servants dealing with economic policy from across the administration found themselves attending multilateral meetings in Brussels. They had to learn quickly that, if progress was to be made on, say, dairying, agreement would also have reached on, say, olive oil and citrus fruit. Success in furthering Irish interests depended on developing new networks and attention to a much wider range of issues than would normally have been considered in Dublin.

This initially posed problems for what was a relatively small civil service, in which each individual official had to cover a wide range of issues. Larger countries could afford to employ many more specialized staff. However, the intellectual stimulus of coming to grips with a range of different approaches and exposure to different models of organizing economies influenced Irish policy development in a way that is difficult to quantify but is acknowledged by all participants as having been important.

It was not just the public administration which was affected by EU member-ship. The social partners, trade unions and employers, also had to learn new approaches. As a legacy of Ireland's membership of the UK, many of the Irish trade unions were branches of UK unions and, as such, followed very much in the UK tradition of industrial relations. Partly as a result of this, Ireland suffered from a rather fractious industrial relations scene in the 1970s.

Watching the industrial strife in the UK during the Thatcher years, though, Irish trade union leaders learnt to avoid UK approaches that were damaging trade union interests. In addition, through their participation in the EU Economic and Social Committee, they met trade unionists from across the EU. There they learned that there were other ways of managing industrial relations, which produced better outcomes for their members, involving less strife. The same cultural changes affected employers and their organizations, which participated with the trade unions in the EU Economic and Social Committee, and in the National Economic and Social Council (NESC), estab-lished in 1973.

The result was a change in approach over the 1980s, leading to reduced industrial relations problems at a time when there was a severe fiscal adjust-ment. Without such changes in approach, the pain of the fiscal adjustment of those years could have evoked major additional economic disruption with a significant cost for employees and employers.

In 1987 this change in approach was formalized in an agreement between employers, trade unions and government to change public policy. It involved reducing the tax burden, in return for agreed moderation in wage demands. This agreement reflected the reality in the labour market where much of the ultimate incidence of taxes on labour fell more on employers than employees (FitzGerald 1999). As a result, the reduction in taxes on labour also benefitted employers, enhancing competitiveness and contributing to the turnaround in economic fortunes in the 1990s.

The shared, but constrained, approach to social partnership was loosened in the early years of the new millennium, creating vulnerabilities that were exposed by the financial crisis, but the more consensual approach to industrial relations that was built in the late 1980s continues to the present day.

Europe had less of an impact on unsavoury corners of business ethics in Ireland (including improper relations between some prominent business leaders and politicians).[13]

Micro-economic Policies

The EU has been chiefly a regulatory polity, relying heavily on an evolving legal framework designed to support and govern a competitive market economy. The Treaties that underpin European Law have been approved as part of Irish Constitutional Law in a series of referenda put to the people at each Treaty revision. The microeconomic policies of the Union, consistent with the Treaties, are given effect through Directives (which are to be transposed into national law) and Regulations (which have direct effect throughout the Union).

The structure of Irish law is based on the traditions of English Common Law, whose approach differs quite significantly from that in most of the other EU countries. But this has not been an obstacle to the Directives being duly transposed into Irish law. By now, much of the legal and regulatory regime governing economic activity in Ireland is a transposition of EU law.

As a result, when trade, industrial and regulatory policies are decided at EU level, the pressures from sectoral special interests, which could otherwise distort national policy away from the common good, are removed from the national political arena.

This does not mean that the legal and regulatory regime has been pulled away from some national model by adherence to the Union; instead, what has happened is that the elaboration and adaptation of law, that would in any case have been needed to cope with the changing technology of business, has been outsourced to the legislative structures of the Union – structures in which Ireland has, of course, a voice. To be sure, some laws and regulations will not

---

[13] Byrne (2012) provides an account, to which the evidence exposed in several court cases following the financial crisis could be added. See also O'Toole (2021).

have been ideally adapted to Irish conditions, but the fact of harmonization within the Union – and often to a model which parallels microeconomic policy trends under way in non-European jurisdictions – generates a degree of certainty and convenience which, for Ireland, largely outweighs any losses.

The remit of the EU Commission is concentrated on developing and implementing policies in areas of economic and social activity which have an important cross-border dimension, while policy areas such as education and health have remained primarily a national responsibility. Here we look at three selected areas of microeconomic policy where European law has influenced the evolution of Irish economic activity, namely competition, energy and the environment and climate. In each case, EU membership has improved Irish economic performance, but in each case Irish practice falls short of the optimum.

Competition

Before Ireland joined the EU, much of the manufacturing sector was dominated by firms that had been established under protection to supply the domestic market. They had not sought to expand by competing on export markets. Given the small size of the Irish market, many of these businesses were de facto sole monopoly suppliers for Irish consumers, with protection preventing competition from outside Ireland. This resulted in low productivity levels, and it allowed firms to charge higher margins. For example, as discussed in Section 2, under protection cars, nearly all of which were imported, had to be disassembled ('completely knocked-down', or CKD) before they were imported and then rebuilt. This was exceptionally inefficient, resulting in high prices, and also giving rise to quality control problems.[14]

This changed with the opening of the Irish market to competition after EU entry. Since then, competition from external suppliers has been essential in keeping downward pressure on prices. For many products all supply comes from outside Ireland.

However, as an island, the physical separation of the Irish market from other EU markets has contributed to higher price levels. Transport costs, and the time that it takes to dispatch goods from continental Europe, have particularly impacted competition in the food retail sector.

EU competition policy, while important, has had a limited impact on the Irish economy because of the generally small size of Irish-owned firms (Mitchell and

---

[14] All car assembly work had closed by 1980, being replaced by imports. But it was noted that FDI had brought the entry of firms producing various components used in the motor industry and which provided more employment than the CKD business ever had.

O'Toole 2021). Domestic competition policy developed in the model of EU legislation, but has played a minor role in changing firms' behaviour, partly because competition from outside Ireland is so important.[15]

It is in the domestic services sector, where a range of factors limit the scope for competition from outside Ireland, that especially significant issues of monopoly and restrictive practices remain. In discussing policy conditions for the financial support during the financial crisis, the EU Commission focused on the need for reform in the provision of legal services in Ireland, but it had limited success.

Banking is a sector where competition has significantly weakened following the financial crisis. Cross-border retail banking in Europe has contracted, several foreign banks have withdrawn from the Irish market and just three domestic retail banks remain active.

EU competition policy plays a bigger role in trying to manage the oligopolistic forces in markets served by some of the multinational firms operating in Ireland, especially those in the information services sector. To date, even in this sector, EU competition policy has not been especially effective.

The establishment of the EU Single Market from the late 1980s began to open up public procurement across the EU, ensuring that all EU firms competed on an equal footing for contracts, wherever they were based. This was a clear net positive for Ireland, given the small size of the national procurement relative to what was being opened up across the Union.

Until the Single Market came into force, supplies of a range of high-tech products tended to be provided to the public sector of larger EU members from national firms. For example, telecommunications equipment in Germany was provided by Siemens and in France by CIT-Alcatel. A similar situation existed in other areas, such as some aspects of pharmaceuticals. The huge expansion of production in the Irish pharmaceuticals sector since the early 1990s is partly attributable to this newly available market in the EU; and Irish-made pharmaceutical exports have continued to grow into the global market. At least initially, there was also an expansion in the production of telecommunications equipment to supply the EU market; since 2000 the telecommunications equipment market has been subsumed into the wider global IT equipment market.

Energy

The 2022 war in Ukraine highlighted the limitations of EU policy in achieving a secure and integrated energy market. On a smaller scale, the long-standing

---

[15] Because of the presence in Ireland of the European headquarters of several globally important information services firms, though, the Irish authority is de facto a lead regulator of data protection for the EU.

challenge of improving integration of Irish electricity with the rest of the EU remains a work-in-progress, with recent setbacks resulting from Brexit.

The development of a Single Electricity Market (SEM) on the island of Ireland, beginning in 2007, successfully provided an integrated market covering the island of Ireland, despite the fact that Northern Ireland is part of the UK. This required joint legislation in the British and Irish parliaments to establish the legal framework.

At first, there was not much electricity trade between the island of Ireland market and the Great Britain (GB) market, because of the way the SEM had been structured. There were, for example, differences in the time horizon of the trades in the two markets which could lead to electricity sometimes perversely flowing from the more expensive to the cheaper market. Because of this, and in order to facilitate trade, a change was made in the SEM's structure in 2017. This change was required under EU law and came into force just before Brexit. However, Brexit has not affected the operation of this market.

The technical links between the Irish and the GB electricity markets are weak. Furthermore, after Brexit, Ireland currently has no direct connection to the continental EU market. However, as part of a wider programme of strengthening internal electricity transmission links within the EU, a new interconnector to France is to be completed later in this decade. Approximately 50 per cent of the cost of this interconnector is being funded directly by the EU. So, for Ireland, despite the longer distance, it is cost competitive relative to connection to GB. In the case of the existing two interconnectors with GB, all of the cost was paid for by Irish consumers.

Increased interconnection is important to facilitate the rapid growth in the generation of renewable electricity. Already, when it is windy in Ireland, there can be an excess supply of renewable electricity, which cannot be used or exported, and this is likely to occur more frequently over time. At least as important, when the wind is not blowing the price of electricity in Ireland often rises above that on neighbouring EU markets, which would make imports profitable and reduce overall carbon emissions.

For a couple of decades, most of Irish gas supplies came from domestic offshore fields. Currently, though, Ireland receives 70 per cent of its gas either from the UK or at least through the UK. While the UK remained an EU member, the high level of gas connection to GB provided security against temporary interruption. After Brexit the UK is no longer governed by EU rules, which could leave Ireland potentially vulnerable to changes in UK policy on gas supplies. Still, there are bilateral Ireland–UK agreements which provide a degree of certainty on supplies. In addition, because of the integrated nature of gas and electricity supplies on the island of Ireland, it would be difficult to treat Ireland differently from Northern Ireland, which is, of course, part of the UK.

Environment and Climate

Agricultural interests have tended to push Ireland into the camp of 'foot draggers' in regard to the evolution of EU environmental legislation over the years (Laffan and O'Mahony 2008). Nevertheless, EU legislation has had some impact, even if Ireland's current situation, in regard to both water quality and greenhouse gas emissions, falls well short of objectives.

Initially, some types of cross-border pollution, both air and water, were subject to EU legislation. The regulations to reduce emissions of sulphur dioxide were put in place over thirty years ago. That was because emissions of this gas from combustion in one country turned into acid rain falling in other countries and causing significant damage there (McCoy 1991; Newbery et al. 1990). This legislation forced firms across the EU, including in Ireland, to implement measures to end such emissions.

Another area on which the EU initially focused attention was pollution of the sea from a range of sources, including urban sewerage. This reflected the fact that in relatively closed seas, such as the Mediterranean, the North Sea and the Baltic Sea, pollution emanating from one country was impacting on the quality of life in neighbouring countries bordering on the sea. The Urban Waste Water Directive aimed to eliminate such pollution and the cross-border damage that it was causing.

Damage caused to neighbouring countries by sea pollution created in Ireland is more limited, given the wider expanse of the receiving waters around Ireland, especially the Atlantic Ocean. Nevertheless, the Urban Waste Water Directive entailed substantial investment (partly funded by the EU) in remedial works in Ireland.

Because of the priority given to potential cross-border effects, a lower priority was given by EU legislation to tackling pollution of rivers and lakes. As a result, while much of the pollution of the coastal waters has been eliminated, the quality of water in Irish rivers and lakes remains a serious issue, one that EU legislation covering agriculture aims to reduce or eliminate over the coming decade.

With growing awareness during the 1990s of the major threat from anthropogenic global warming, the Commission initially proposed a common carbon/energy tax to apply to all EU members to reduce emissions. However Ireland, along with a number of other countries, opposed this proposed tax, partly out of concerns for any policy innovation involving a harmonized approach to taxation. Since then the EU has gradually developed a suite of alternative policies to tackle climate change.

The Emissions Trading Scheme (ETS), which has been in place for fifteen years, has seen a reduction in emissions across the EU from the sectors covered (mainly power stations, large energy using plants and airlines). However, the scheduled emissions reductions were too limited and the price of permits was too low. Reforms have subsequently resulted in higher prices, driving change in Ireland and elsewhere.

For the emissions not covered by the ETS scheme, the EU established national limits. In 2010 Ireland had already introduced a modest carbon tax of €20 a tonne on emissions of carbon dioxide from energy use by non-ETS sectors. However, while most EU members met their target for reducing emissions by 2020, Ireland failed to do so despite the carbon tax, and despite the slowdown in economic activity resulting from the financial crisis.

The EU has set emissions limits for the non-ETS sector for each member state for the period to 2030. These limits will be further tightened as a result of the increased ambition for action agreed at the EU level. In 2021 Ireland adopted its own national limits, which are more stringent than the EU's existing limits, and likely to be at least as ambitious as the revised EU limits. It remains to be seen whether domestic policies are put in place to realize the necessary reduction.

The Irish government has agreed to a gradual ramping up of the national carbon tax each year to reach €100 per tonne in 2030. This is one national instrument to drive change, but significant additional measures will be needed if the EU targets for emissions reduction are to be met. If the EU proposals to extend the ETS scheme to cover emissions from transport and heat are implemented it could ensure that, at least at the level of the EU, the target for emissions reduction would be met. However, the disruptions arising from the Ukraine war complicate the situation.

Contrasts with Northern Ireland

The fortunes of the economy of Northern Ireland have fluctuated in quite different ways to that of the Republic. Overall, during the period of EU membership, economic growth and productivity in Northern Ireland fell well below that in the Republic – and below most of the rest of the UK.

With a population of only 3 per cent of the UK (and now less than two-fifths that of the Republic), Northern Ireland is a relatively small component of the UK, but it has had a devolved government since the 1920s, albeit with some interruptions when the political or security situation led to periods of direct rule from London. Most economic matters are devolved – though not currency and little of taxation – but Northern Ireland benefits from substantial fiscal support from the UK Government.

Just as in the Republic, EU legislation applied to Northern Ireland until 2020. Its agriculture sector operated under the CAP, and, as an 'Objective 1' region, it received EU Structural Funds, including under the Interreg cross-border funding programme. An important consequence of EU membership, and especially the EU Single Market, was that the land border on the island of Ireland became economically seamless. But the administrative relationship of Northern Ireland with Europe was largely mediated through London, and did not involve the wholesale repositioning of external economic relations that took place south of the border.

It would be a mistake to assign too much of the contrasting economic development of the two jurisdictions on the island to differences in their relationship with Europe. It is not hard to point to reasons for the relatively weak economic performance of Northern Ireland during the period under review. The structure of that region's economy had long been different from that of the rest of the island. Like the North of England and Scotland a powerhouse of shipbuilding, textiles and other manufacturing sectors, Northern Ireland suffered deindustrialization as emerging economies captured market share in these sectors. Furthermore, economic progress north of the border in the early decades of EU membership was blighted by decades of civil unrest and terrorism until the 1998 political settlement. Despite the troubles, some FDI was attracted to Northern Ireland by a regime of grants, but the US connection was less prominent, and, not being tax-driven, many of the firms that did come were not in rapidly growing and profitable sectors.

Other economic policy choices have also slowed Northern Ireland's economic development over the past half century. Spending on economic infrastructures fell behind that elsewhere in the UK, and educational attainment also fell behind, recording proportionately more early school leavers and fewer workers with third-level qualifications than in other UK regions (FitzGerald and Morgenroth 2020). These too are dimensions not directly affected by EU policies or legislation.

Management of Northern Ireland's macroeconomic stability over the years was largely out of its own hands. That was not true for the Republic, which stumbled badly in this respect, though in each case recovering after a period of necessary adjustment, as is discussed in Section 5.

5 Macroeconomic Volatility

Ireland's macroeconomic experience in the half-century of European membership has been chequered. EU exchange rate regimes and the rules on budget balance played a part, but significant domestic policy mistakes drove two cycles of over-expansion and recession. Ineffective macroeconomic policy delayed Ireland's achievement of full employment and its aggregate progress towards the efficient production frontier. Eventually, though, the Irish economy displayed a stronger average growth profile than ever before, and converged to be among the leading group of EU countries in terms of prosperity.

If the structure of production in Ireland was strongly influenced by the movement to free trade in goods and services, macroeconomic fluctuations have been more related to the freedom of capital movements.

Capital moved freely also before EU membership; mostly outward, as Irish banks placed surplus funds in the London money market, because capital mobility between Ireland and Britain was also unrestricted before 1978. And after 1992 freedom of capital movements extended to the EU as a whole.

The combination of capital and labour mobility, both de jure and de facto, has given the Irish economy some of the characteristics of a regional as well as a national economy. The main factors of production, labour and capital, can adapt quickly and at scale to changing opportunities and business confidence. Sometimes this elasticity amplifies shocks; sometimes it absorbs them. The net result has been a major reason why the Irish economy has displayed greater macroeconomic volatility than many other EU countries.

Europe's role in colouring Ireland's macroeconomic stability has come through the rules and vicissitudes of the two exchange rate mechanisms: the European Monetary System (EMS) from 1979 to about 1993, and the European Monetary Union (EMU) in the past quarter century. These mechanisms changed the context within which the consequences of domestic macroeconomic policy choices would be felt, both for good and for ill.

Tough Initial Years: Stagflation in the 1970s

No sooner had Ireland joined the EU than it, like all European countries, was hit by the oil price crisis of 1973, which cast a pall over economic performance for the first few years of membership. The increased competition in the goods market and rising Irish wage rates (discussed in earlier sections) added to job losses and firm closures. Unemployment also grew in the UK, so it provided no cushion to soften the growth in Irish unemployment. Despite the high unemployment in Ireland, for several years net migration was inward, something that had not happened for a century and a half.

The UK inflationary spiral that followed the 1973 oil shock transmitted fully into Irish prices, as was inevitable in view of the fixed one-for-one peg between the British and Irish currencies. In both countries, annual inflation peaked at well over 20 per cent in 1975. Even though imported inflation was unavoidable, there was much soul-searching and industrial unrest as trade unions pushed hard to ensure that wages kept up with the cost of living and restored or improved traditional relativities with those in Britain. The Irish Government even introduced (briefly) a small subsidy on imported potatoes in order to prevent the measured Consumer Price Index from passing a certain threshold that would have triggered an agreed step-up in centrally negotiated wages! Growing awareness that the imported inflation could not be effectively tackled with such measures began to fuel dissatisfaction with the Irish exchange rate regime.

Meanwhile, the recession of the 1970s took its toll on the public finances. Previously committed to balancing the current budget, the Government had already planned a small current deficit for 1972 – even before the oil price rise. Ireland followed the UK in seeking to cushion the impact of the downturn using fiscal measures. By 1975, the general government deficit approached 20 per cent of GNP, of which about 4 percentage points reflected debt servicing charges, so that the primary deficit was about 16 per cent of GDP. Now the policy shifted to correcting the deficit. The 1976 Budget was probably the most deflationary of recent times. The attempt to do so through unprecedented fiscal austerity saw unemployment continuing to climb in 1976 (Figure 16; Kearney 2012; Kearney et al. 2000).

Widespread dissatisfaction with economic performance had the result that a new government was elected in 1977 on an ill-fated campaign to tackle unemployment through tax cuts and spending increases. This dash for growth expanded public investment spending and employment in the public sector. A relaxed official approach to wage claims also increased public spending to unaffordable levels. Unemployment did respond favourably at first, but the

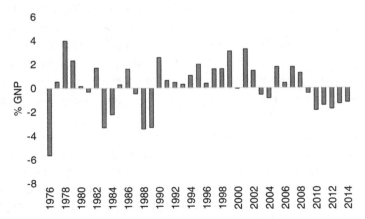

Figure 16 Fiscal impulse 1976–2014

Source: Authors' calculations based on Kearney (2012).

increased economic activity was not strong enough to prevent the fiscal imbalance from continuing to deteriorate.

Europe as such had little direct role in the macroeconomic and fiscal policy decisions of these bleak years. Macroeconomic policy surveillance was not yet part of the European project, and, agriculture aside, EU policies still had a relatively small direct role in the Irish economy.

The Fiscal Crisis of the 1980s

The attempt to use fiscal expansion to jump-start an employment recovery from 1977 soon degenerated into a fiscal crisis. The 1976–7 improvement in the public finances was quickly reversed and borrowing continued to grow, not least following the second oil price shock and the tightening of fiscal and monetary policy in Britain and the US. After years of being negative, real interest rates, on the growing wave of debt refinancing, turned sharply positive. With job opportunities scarce in the UK, unemployment in Ireland soon began to increase rapidly again.

A change of government in 1981 promised to correct the deterioration in the public finances. Its attempts, primarily through tax rate increases, were not maintained with sufficient perseverance and proved unsuccessful. The tax increases damaged business and consumer confidence, deepening the economic malaise. Higher world interest rates now interacted with a loss of investor confidence to increase the cost of Government borrowing, which was now running at unprecedented levels. As a result, although the General Government Borrowing peaked in 1982 at 12½ per cent of GDP, it was still in double digits in 1986, having averaged more than 10 per cent for a decade (Honohan 1999). At this point, the sustainability of Ireland's debt, which had reached almost 120 per cent of GNP, was being widely called into question (FitzGerald and Kenny 2018). About a half of this debt was either denominated in foreign currency or held by foreign entities. Bringing the fiscal deficit under control was not a matter of choice but one of constraint: 'austerity' was not chosen but imposed out of necessity. In all of this, official Europe had no direct role, positive or negative.

Unemployment also peaked in 1986 at over 17 per cent – an all-time record. Subsequently it eased back a little, as labour market conditions in Britain started to improve. Other external factors also moved more favourably. Lower real and nominal international interest rates passed through to the Government's cost of borrowing. And (with membership of the EMS having replaced the sterling link, as described below) exchange rate movements lowered the value of the Irish pound, especially relative to sterling.

After 1987, recognition of the need for more thorough fiscal correction had become politically bipartisan: budget deficits narrowed sharply from 1988 (Figure 16). Market participants quickly realized that the new political configuration had the determination to correct the situation and sentiment improved. Against the background of an improving industrial relations environment (as mentioned in Section 4), a series of national pay agreements achieved pay restraint in return for progressive reductions in the burden of income tax. The output and employment response (and eventually the inflow of EU Structural Funds) ensured that these tax commitments could be delivered, even as the public finances dramatically improved and the ratio of Government debt to GNI fell sharply. Soon the fiscal crisis had been overcome, though, with a further uptick in UK unemployment in the early 1990s, Irish unemployment did not fall below 10 per cent until 1998.

Looking at the geography of these developments, it is again clear that, two decades into EU membership, fluctuations in Ireland's macroeconomic conditions still depended more on the UK than they did on Continental Europe.

Ireland's Currency Choices in Europe

Currency policy provides another example of how Ireland sought to use its new EU partnership to escape economic dependence on Britain. Despite having adhered to a one-for-one currency peg with the pound sterling for over 150 years, Ireland opted to break this link and to join the two successive currency regimes introduced in Europe in 1979 and 1999.

The EMS, with its grid of bilateral exchange rate pegs and intervention limits, was agreed in 1978 as part of the decision by France to re-enter a stable exchange rate relationship with Germany. A political push was made to include the pound sterling in the new system, but the British Government demurred, participating only in a detached manner, and sterling did not adhere to the Exchange Rate Mechanism (ERM) of the system.

Britain's reluctance to join the ERM presented a difficult policy choice for Ireland. On the one hand this was an opportunity to come out from under a currency link that had recently been delivering high inflation rates. On the other hand a link to the deutschemark was likely to prove deflationary and the Irish labour market might not be ready for the degree of wage restraint needed to remain competitive in such a system.

In the end, Ireland negotiated a useful package of grants and loans designed to ease the adjustment, and it decided to join the system (Honohan and Murphy 2010). As the start date approached, the Irish authorities became worried about the danger of destabilizing speculative capital movements, now that the sterling link was under threat and given the long tradition of fully free financial connections between Britain and Ireland. Accordingly they introduced strict exchange controls between Ireland and the UK.

Thus, a move towards stronger links with part of the European Community had the effect of breaking important links with the UK. Within just a few weeks, exchange rate fluctuations meant that the sterling link became incompatible with the intervention obligations of the new system, and had to be abandoned.

Soon there was a silver lining, when the monetary tightening introduced by the British Government, along with fiscal austerity, saw the market value of the pound sterling appreciate strongly during 1979 and 1980. No longer tied to sterling, Ireland was sheltered from what would have been a significant loss of competitiveness in the early years of the ERM – a time when, as we have seen, economic conditions were extremely weak.

Nevertheless, the ERM proved to be quite an unsatisfactory regime, both in general and in particular for Ireland. Despite its declared ambition to be a 'zone of monetary stability', realignments of the pegs and intervention limits were more frequent than had been anticipated – about one a year in the first seven years. Ireland took advantage of several of these realignments to avoid an excessive appreciation, especially against sterling; in particular, responding to a weakening of sterling in the previous months, Ireland secured a unilateral 10 per cent devaluation in August 1986.

The frequency of realignments in the ERM made the exchange rate peg of financially weaker countries vulnerable to speculative pressure, resulting in high interest rates. Indeed, holders of Irish pound monetary assets realized a substantial premium over German assets (about 2½ per cent per annum between 1983 and 1993) during the ERM period, implying that the interest rate differential was far higher than needed to compensate for actual exchange rate depreciation in these years (Figure 17).

Shortly after the UK belatedly decided to join the ERM in 1990, exchange market tensions in the system increased, partly associated with the financial consequences of Germany's unification.[16] In the last few months of 1992, speculative flows forced several countries, including the UK, out of the system. The sharp depreciation of sterling which followed its exit attracted strong speculation against the Irish pound. This was resisted for a time by the Central Bank of Ireland with extremely high short-term interest rates, before the decision to devalue once more at the end of January 1993. A few months

---

[16] Responding to inflationary pressures, the Bundesbank brought its policy interest rates to unusually high levels in 1990–1. This tightening of monetary policy was transmitted through the EMS to other countries, with a negative impact on the Irish economy already apparent in 1991 (Bradley et al. 1991).

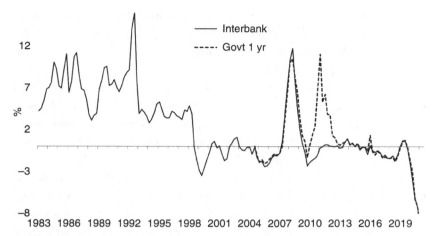

Figure 17 Realized real wholesale interest rates 1983–2021 Interbank rate and
1-year Government bond yield deflated by 4-quarter future inflation

Source: Authors' calculation based on Central Bank of Ireland.

later, with pressure still being experienced, notably on the French franc, the ERM was practically dissolved, with the allowable fluctuation margins increased to plus or minus 15 per cent.

The continued special importance of the British connection was a constant theme in Ireland's experience with the EMS. While few thought that the sterling peg could or should be re-established, it was clear that the exchange rate relationship with Britain could not be ignored in formulating exchange rate policy for Ireland in Europe. This concern with the sterling exchange rate reflected the degree to which the chief competitors of indigenous Irish producers of tradable goods were still in Britain.

It was not long before this issue became central. Already before the ERM crisis, plans were well advanced to replace the unsatisfactory multi-currency adjustable peg system with a common European currency managed by a supranational European Central Bank (ECB).

Should Ireland join this system? By adopting the proposed new currency, Ireland would no longer have the tool of devaluation available to it in order to counter the competitiveness consequences of a bout of sterling weakness. The new regime would be a kind of straitjacket on certain aspects of Ireland's economic policy.

Furthermore, in the eyes of some, the promise of a single European currency was a chimaera: any such regime might not really differ much from an old-fashioned exchange rate peg – the threat of a country's exit might mean that national interest rates could still be subject to a currency risk premium.

If it worked well, though, the single currency could offer an escape from the high real interest rate differentials that had been experienced by Ireland in the ERM, and which persisted, albeit at narrower levels, in the floating period that followed the collapse of the ERM.

Once again, the Irish Government's decision was to stay with the main thrust of European integration in the financial sphere. The Maastricht Treaty, initiating the creation of a single currency, had already been passed by referendum before the ERM crisis, and, doubts about the economic advantages notwithstanding, Ireland became a founder adopter of the euro from the start of 1999.

The optimists' view on interest rate differentials proved to be justified for the first decade of the euro. For a country with such recent experience of high interest rates and an over-indebted government, the sharply lower interest rates were welcomed. The new currency began with a weak tone against sterling and the US dollar, and this added to Irish inflation and resulted in real interest rates that were even lower than those being experienced elsewhere in the euro area (Honohan and Lane 2003). But soon the easier conditions began to encourage increasingly unsound spending conditions, public and private.

The Construction Bubble and Bust

It was not just euro area membership that put virtually unlimited borrowed funds at the disposal of Irish banks, though it may have helped given that there was no longer any national exchange rate risk involved. These were years of global financialization. That provided an opportunity, but it was mishandled, with dramatic consequences. This time, the EU played an important part in how the ensuing crisis was handled.

EU rules about fiscal and macroeconomic policy really came into their own for the first time for euro area membership. The famous Maastricht criteria, defining ceilings for General Government debt at 60 per cent of GDP, the borrowing requirement at 3 per cent of GDP and real interest rates close to the average of other member states, were widely criticized by economists for lacking a robust evidential basis to support the proposition that violation of these criteria would destabilize the single currency regime.

The political driver for these rules was the fear in the countries with recent experience of persistent surpluses and an appreciating currency, especially Germany and the Netherlands, that the new regime would drag them into inflation and transfers to assist countries such as Italy whose recent history was marked by exchange rate depreciation and deficits.

Actually, although some commentators pointed to the Maastricht criteria as having steered Ireland to a disciplined fiscal stance in the 1990s, the deficit ratio was already satisfied in Ireland by the time the Maastricht Treaty was ratified, and the debt ratio was well on the way to being satisfied.

Indeed the late 1990s saw Ireland's macroeconomy in a more healthy and balanced condition than at any time since independence, with a rapid export-driven rate of output and employment growth based on improvements in competitiveness, and public finances dramatically improved. This 'Celtic Tiger' attracted much attention among new and prospective EU member states, and more widely as other countries sought to emulate this apparent success.

It is therefore remarkable that, within a decade, independent Ireland faced the most severe economic and fiscal crisis of its history, with both the banking system and the Government looking at insolvency in the face, despite having adhered to the European fiscal criteria and with the various pieces of European legislation governing banking regulation.

What happened in Ireland revealed the superficial nature of the rules that had been set by Europe and showed how relying exclusively on overly simple rules could allow an unstable and fragile financial structure to emerge.

From about 2000, the process of Irish convergence to the European frontier of productivity and full employment was approaching its culmination. This process could no longer be expected to drive economic growth at the rates that had been experienced since the mid-1990s. But the existence of such a ceiling was not recognized either by property developers, their bankers, or by the institutions of Government, whether at home or at the European level (Ó Gráda 2002).

Responding to rising housing and office prices both in Ireland and abroad, Irish property developers sought and received bank funding for massive construction projects. Competing among themselves for the growing market share that seemed to drive the prices of their equity, banks were eager to expand this seemingly profitable business. And they could do so, without having to add much to their equity buffers, because of the glut of global savings which was sweeping Europe and the world in those years (cf. Everett 2015). That such funds could be made available in euros, now the local currency, may have eased the flow further, though in practice Irish banks' foreign borrowing in sterling and US dollars outweighed their borrowing in euros (Lane 2015).[17]

By financing the household buyers of residential property in Ireland as well as the property developers, the banks in Ireland boosted what was, by 2004, becoming one of the strongest credit-fuelled price and construction booms seen anywhere in modern history. The share of the workforce engaged in construction jumped from about 7 per cent in the early and mid-1990s to over

---

[17] Note that non-euro European countries, such as Iceland and Latvia, also accessed international finance to generate unsustainable booms in those years. And other euro area countries were also affected by a 'financial resource curse' (Dellepiane-Avellaneda et al. 2021).

13 per cent by 2007. Real housing prices increased by 260 per cent between 1995 and 2006. Meanwhile Irish property developers became conspicuous players in markets as diverse as London, Chicago, Constanta and Cape Verde.

All of the banks operating in the Irish market contributed to the boom. About a third of the domestic-facing part of the Irish banking system was owned and controlled in other EU countries. It was British-owned banks who introduced the 100 per cent mortgage and the tracker mortgage (with a variable interest rate linked to the ECB's policy rate). Belgium, Denmark and the Netherlands were the home countries of three of the other foreign-owned banks operating in the Irish market. (US banks, operating on an offshore basis in the IFSC, did not get involved in the Irish property boom, nor did the German IFSC banks – though these did get into trouble from their US-related operations after 2007.)

The three largest banks were Irish-controlled, but they sourced much of their funding in international financial markets, to which they became heavily indebted, though without this affecting the cost of funds, which were provided at very keen rates – even for risk-taking subordinated debt. It is not easy to pinpoint the extent to which the funding for the Irish property boom came from the rest of the EU rather than the rest of the world, as such geographic distinctions were not central to the thinking of bankers or their regulators in those days.

There was nothing much in the way of red flags on banking issues from EU institutions as the bubble expanded. It was only in 2007 that warning signs on the condition of the banks began to be recognized in official circles: the source of Irish banks' foreign funding was shrinking geographically to the UK and its maturity shortening (cf. Lane 2015).

In those years, no European institution had supervisory jurisdiction over banks – this having been largely omitted from the legislation that created the ECB. European legislation had established capital adequacy requirements, but these were to be enforced at the national level, even though a banking license granted in one member state empowered a bank to operate throughout the EU.

Besides, the calculation of bank capital in a property price bubble tended to neglect the degree to which the recoverable value of loans made on property could collapse. This was the Achilles heel of the capital-adequacy-based approach to prudential supervision of banks. Unless bank management, auditors or the supervisor recognized that there was an increased risk of a collapse in the valuation of bank assets, a bank's true ability to weather prospective problems tended to be overstated. Ireland's banks reported levels of risk-taking capital well in excess of regulatory requirements, and, although the supervisory authority did insist in 2006 on some add-ons to the EU standards in respect of speculative property loans, these add-ons were marginal and well within the levels of capital already being reported by the banks.

In fiscal matters, there was some EU jurisdiction; the Council did, at the suggestion of the Commission, issue a Recommendation to Ireland over its budget for 2001 which it saw as contributing to overheating and as such inconsistent with the Broad Economic Policy Guidelines; but it did not persist in this view, despite its solid foundation (cf. Alesina et al. 2001). Because the economy was growing rapidly the government ran a surplus in six of the seven years between 2001 and 2007, fully complying with the Stability and Growth Pact which succeeded the Maastricht criteria, even though most of the budget measures adopted in those years were stimulatory in nature (Figure 16). But that surplus was heavily dependent on what would prove to be evanescent revenues coming from the property bubble. The over-simple Maastricht criteria had made no provision for revenue transience or volatility. Increasingly insistent words of caution by domestic commentators were ignored.

When the Irish property bubble reversed, the sudden stop in construction, combined with the external demand shock from the GFC, pushed the banking system into insolvency and almost fatally weakened the public finances, which had been heavily supported by what would prove to be ephemeral property-boom related taxes such as corporation and capital gains taxes and stamp duties (Figure 18). For a banking system that had been riding so high, and a Government that had been running surpluses for so long in a rapidly

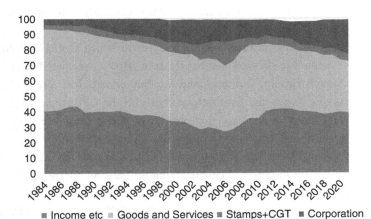

Figure 18 Composition of tax revenue, 1984–2022 (%). CGT is capital gains tax.

Source: Department of Finance.

growing economy that its debt-to-GDP ratio had reached as low as 24 per cent, the shock was severe and unexpected.[18]

Now EU institutions became centrally involved. The Irish Government was reprimanded for introducing a blanket guarantee on bank liabilities at the end of September 2008, because of the pressure for emulation that it created.[19] Despite the guarantee, the Irish banks struggled to source market funding to replace maturing deposits and bonds: more and more of their funding was provided by the ECB and, when the banks ran out of eligible collateral for the ECB's normal financing facilities (even though the criteria had been eased), the Irish-controlled banks all had to have recourse to emergency liquidity assistance (ELA) from the national central bank. This lender-of-last-resort function could only be exercised if the ECB did not object. As reliance on ELA increased, the ECB's willingness to do so came under stress.

The reason that the Irish Government's guarantee was not sufficient to ensure funding for the banks was that the sustainability of its own finances had come into question as a result of the sharp reduction in tax revenue, the additional cost of unemployment support and the cost of recapitalizing the Irish banks. All in all, these pressures resulted in a borrowing requirement in 2010 reaching 32 per cent of GDP, a level which alarmed financial markets.

How would the EU respond to this acute financial and economic crisis in a member state? To a considerable extent the response was influenced by (i) the fact that Greece had also fallen into a financial crisis; (ii) the prospect of other countries following suit, most obviously Portugal, but also potentially Italy and Spain and (iii) the weak economic conditions more generally resulting from the GFC.

At the time, and also in retrospect, the degree to which the EU exhibited solidarity in supporting stressed member states in 2010–11 seemed disappointing. Even though Britain, Germany and the Netherlands had also suffered alarming banking losses and fiscal stresses early in the GFC, their relatively faster recovery led to a narrative that prioritized blame over rescue for the stressed countries, and emphasized moral hazard as a reason for caution in providing financial assistance. While this was not unjustifiable, it led to a slower recovery, not just for the stressed countries, but for the euro area as a whole as investors hedged against contagion risks. The existential threat to the euro persisted until the convincing announcement of ECB President Mario Draghi

---

[18] Indeed, that figure is double the net debt, considering the foreign assets held by the Government's reserve fund.

[19] Despite what is said in many secondary sources, there is no evidence whatsoever that Europe encouraged Ireland to introduce the bank guarantee (Honohan 2019; Oireachtas 2016).

in July 2012. Worst affected was Greece, which would have performed better had the debt restructuring happened earlier and affected more of Greece's debt.

For Ireland, once it had lost market access to financing at reasonable rates of interest (a process not unaffected by various statements by leading EU policy-makers), the solution adopted was the correct one of accessing official financing until market confidence could be restored. The ad hoc consortium of the European Commission and the IMF, in association with the ECB (known colloquially as the *Troika*), which had been formed in mid-2010 for the financing of Greece, was pressed into service again for Ireland. About two-thirds of the needed funding was provided by euro area funds, and there were bilateral contributions from Denmark and the UK, so the Commission took the lead formally – though for the design of policy conditionality heavy reliance was placed in practice on the IMF.

While the financial assistance programme was ultimately successful, its initial design can be criticized on at least three grounds. Firstly, the rate of interest charged was too high to ensure debt sustainability. Secondly, the still unquantified risks embedded in the banking system remained with the Irish Government, which was obliged to inject additional capital reserves into the banks, based on a new stress test. The lenders could more easily have absorbed these risks, for example by providing insurance or buying equity themselves in the restructured banks, instead of lending the Irish Government the money to buy the equity. Thirdly, an apparent conflict of interest lay in the ECB's participation, as it was not providing any new funds, but had a strong interest to ensure that the outlays it had already made to the Irish banking system were repaid.

Each of these problems was later mitigated. The interest rate on the European loans was lowered in mid-2011 to little more than Europe's cost of funds. (This was largely in parallel with a redesign of the Greek programme, which would not have worked at the high interest rates.) The banking stress test carried out in Ireland in 2011 proved to be sufficiently conservative in terms of loan losses that the Government did not have to inject any additional capital into the three largest banks after mid-2011. And the ECB eventually acquiesced in a resolution of the ELA banking debts on financial terms that proved very favourable to Ireland (Honohan 2019).

Governments in the larger European countries and elsewhere moved too quickly in 2010 to a post-crisis policy of fiscal adjustment (or 'austerity'). Ireland had no choice but to follow suit. As in the 1980s, the government's dependence on foreign borrowing meant that the adjustment could not be delayed any further than permitted by the scale of the bailout funds and the need to recover financial market access at reasonable cost. Clearly, these constraints limited the government's immediate ability to support aggregate demand. Responding to the sharp decline in tax receipts when the property bubble collapsed, successive Irish Governments raised tax rates, reduced public sector salaries and some rates of social welfare and cut or postponed expenditure programmes in the period 2008–14.

The confidence of leading Irish figures, whether in politics, public administration or business affairs, was shaken by the financial crisis. While there was an understanding by the population that the crisis was due to Irish policy mistakes, there was some resentment about what was seen as overbearing behaviour by European institutions. But the prevailing sense in official circles was that recovery would require closer attention to Ireland's relations with Europe. And public opinion vis-à-vis the Union soon swung back.

Gradually the state of the public finances improved to the point where, by 2015, Ireland (helped by the asset purchase programme of the ECB) was able to access foreign private funds once more at little over one half of a percentage point above the German Federal Government bond yield.

Economic activity bottomed out in mid-2012, after which Ireland experienced a steady recovery in employment, thanks initially to a recovery in consumer spending and capital formation and later as the fiscal adjustment came to an end. Foreign MNCs, whose trust in the underlying resilience of Irish society had not been lost, continued to add jobs, many of which were taken up by immigrants. The recovery was sustained until the pandemic broke out in 2020 (indeed the previous peak in per capita household consumption was not reached until 2018), and the post-pandemic recovery was also vigorous.

The euro area crisis and Ireland's part in it revealed gaps in the EU's preparedness for collaborative crisis management. It also showed that damaging spill-overs could occur when national banking systems were not well supervised and where national resolution regimes for banking were underdeveloped. The post-crisis creation of the Single Supervisory Mechanism and the Bank Recovery and Resolution Directive were enthusiastically endorsed by Ireland, along with a stronger macroprudential framework.

The report card on how euro membership served Ireland in relation to the crisis is mixed. Euro membership protected Ireland from the surge of inflation that would certainly have accompanied a banking crisis had there been a national currency. But it also shifted the distributional consequences of the collapse. By improving competitiveness, devaluation (such as happened in Iceland, for example) would probably have reduced the fall in the numbers at work, while also reducing the spending power of those who retained their employment. Euro area institutions did help Ireland and other stressed countries, but could have done so more comprehensively and more quickly. Even with hindsight, though, the crisis experience does not suggest that the decision to join the euro was mistaken.

Ireland in Europe without Britain

While it was stated by prominent Irish Government leaders in the 1960s that Ireland would wish to join the Common Market even if Britain did not, that scenario looked unrealistic. But now, fifty years after membership, the United Kingdom has left, but Ireland has stayed – and Eurosceptic voices in Ireland are even scarcer today, especially in the dimension of economic effects.

That is not to say that Brexit has been trouble-free on the economic front for Ireland. For one thing, the introduction of customs and other administrative procedures on Irish trade with Britain creates costs and delays that cannot be neglected. Insofar as is possible such costs are being avoided by routing merchandise trade with the rest of Europe around Britain; there has been a sizable increase in the number and frequency of direct shipping services to continental ports since Brexit. The limited impact also partly reflects the fact that, as yet, the UK has imposed minimal controls on imports.

The adverse macroeconomic effect of Brexit on the UK economy, still a significant market for Irish exporters, is having a dampening effect on Irish economic activity. Several studies estimate that the net adverse medium-term effect on Irish national income of Brexit is likely to be around 5 per cent – coincidentally similar to that estimated for the UK. Disentangling the impact of Brexit from that of the pandemic is, of course, difficult and will take some time. The long-term impact will depend, inter alia, on how UK policy evolves, with a special vulnerability to any move by Britain to seek a low food price policy through trade policy.

Trade with Northern Ireland has in recent years amounted to about 10 per cent of (the Republic of) Ireland's trade with the UK. This is a far higher percentage than the 3 per cent of UK GDP accounted for by Northern Ireland. Indeed – contrary to what is often thought – 'cross-border' trade on the island of Ireland has long been much higher than would be predicted by economists' workhorse model of international trade (Lawless 2019; Lawless et al. 1999). To date, this trade has not been adversely affected by Brexit, thanks to the Protocol.

The destabilizing effect of Brexit on the United Kingdom has raised long-dormant constitutional issues in Northern Ireland. To avoid the imposition of a customs border on the island as a result of the UK leaving the EU, a Protocol governing trade flows was agreed between the UK and the EU. What have motivated the avoidance of a physical customs border on the island are not the trade frictions that it would entail, but the political and security destabilization that would likely follow.

The Protocol in effect leaves significant parts of the Northern Ireland economy still in the EU Single Market, while also remaining part of the UK market. EU checks and customs are, instead, applied at the sea and airports of Northern Ireland for goods arriving there from Britain, imposing some costs on the regional economy, especially the retail sector. Exporting businesses in Northern Ireland retain a degree of access to the EU Single Market no longer available to firms elsewhere in the UK.

However, the fact that there are some checks on trade from Great Britain to Northern Ireland is politically problematic for a significant minority of the population in Northern Ireland.

If the Protocol arrangements do persist into the long term and ensure that there is no economic border on the island of Ireland, they could underpin a strengthening of the island economy, reducing duplication and exploiting economies of scale.

The Irish Economy in Europe Today

By far the poorest country in the European Economic Community on joining, Ireland reached its fiftieth anniversary as one of the more prosperous, even when adjustment is made for the distortions in the GDP accounts.

So, despite setbacks and shortcomings, it has been a strong story of convergence, and one for which EU membership provided key parts of the institutional and policy scaffolding, reinforced when the Customs Union deepened into the Single Market. The Common Agricultural Policy and the Structural Funds fuelled significant resource inflows.

But the economic transformation was also very much a creature of deepening globalization, as Ireland became the export platform of choice for many US and other foreign-owned MNCs, which now account for about half of total tax revenue from the business sector. Indeed, the intensity with which Ireland has embraced globalization is the distinguishing feature of its economic transformation.

It was not all plain sailing. Like the hare in Aesop's fable, Ireland's aggregate economic performance in this half-century has been a sequence of pauses followed by rapid progress. Membership of the EU's two exchange regimes did not protect against poor macroeconomic management. The fiscal crisis of the 1980s mired the economy in unemployment, constrained public services and spiralling taxation. When stability was restored, there was at last a speedy convergence to full employment and towards the international production frontier, strengthened by the increased public investment in education. But a recurrence of macroeconomic and financial policy missteps in the early 2000s meant that Ireland succumbed more severely than most to the GFC from 2008.

EU membership and Ireland's embrace of globalization with an American flavour have also had intangible influences on the way Irish workers, business people, politicians and government officials approach economic decisions.

As well as providing the broad market and regulatory context within which the economy grew, Europe also generated several impulses at key moments: the Single Market just when US multinationals were expanding into the globalizing economy, the Structural Funds just when Ireland was facing an infrastructure and employment deficit. Europe did not help Ireland maintain macroeconomic balance, though it probably did not contribute much to imbalance.

Certainly, as its international economic relations became more diversified within a multilateral European relationship governed by the rule of law, membership of the EU has become increasingly seen in Ireland as a significant advantage, cementing the country's independence much more than constraining its freedom of action.

Membership of the EU has been a bedrock of this evolution, underpinning a coherent and relatively stable overall economic policy framework. But Europe has not determined or limited the path that the Irish economy has followed, nor will it be determinative in the future.

The economic convergence of the 1990s would have been more gradual for an Ireland outside the EU (with its emerging Single Market) and absent the tax inducements for FDI. It would have been impossible had macroeconomic imbalances not been tamed. To which of the other three – EU membership, tax-driven FDI, Single Market – should most credit be given for Ireland's current prosperity?[20]

Considering that it is as a globalized economy that Ireland has developed in these last decades, it is quite imaginable that Ireland could have reached full employment by the turn of the century even if there had been no Single Market. After all, the FDI was flowing well even before then.

But the MNCs would surely not have come in such force if Ireland had not been an EU member with the credibility and market access that membership conveyed. After all, the EU did not prevent Ireland from offering its very attractive corporation tax regime, which played such a large part in attracting FDI.

Is it possible to imagine a prosperous Irish economy within the EU whose productive base relied far more on home-grown companies? The successful Irish MNCs of today suggest that this would not have been impossible. It cannot be the case that reliance on foreign-owned enterprises was the only effective way to broaden access to employment in high-productivity occupations. But the advance would have been quite different, slower and less pronounced.

---

[20] Comparing Ireland's performance with that of matched non-EU countries, the econometric technique used by Campos et al. (2019) suggests that EU membership has been important.

There is no unique formula for success in or out of the EU. The European Union encompasses a broad variety of economic policy regimes, informed by nationally distinctive political and diplomatic characteristics. Europe has provided opportunities and a broad economic policy context within which member states have made varied choices coloured by national pre-conditions.

Other new members of the EU over the past half-century have entered from contrasting starting positions, most of them quite different from where Ireland was at the outset of its membership. For Greece and the two Iberian countries, emergence from authoritarian state regimes defined the evolution of policy in their early years as members. The eleven Central and Eastern European countries were transitioning (in their varied ways) from various forms of the planned economy. The Nordic countries and Austria had already achieved high income levels and were already integrated in the European trading system through their membership in EFTA. And the two Mediterranean island states joined with their unique political and trading histories.

We have shown how Ireland's economic transformation from its previous reliance on the former colonial power to an enthusiastic participant in the global economy has equally been influenced not just by its engagement with the EU, but also (for example) by historical and continuing cultural and economic links with the United States.

It's not as if Ireland's path could have readily been chosen by others. Ireland seized some of the opportunities made available by membership, and learnt much from interacting with a broader range of political, administrative and business actors in Europe. But it did so against its own historical, political and cultural background.

That Ireland made a greater success of its experience in the European economy than several other peripheral countries can be attributed to the greater willingness and ability of Irish people, given their long internationalization experience from migration and from being part of the British Empire, to take advantage of the opportunities offered by globalization and European integration. In addition, they gained from the experience across Northern Europe of the importance of investing in human capital.

The pandemic shock of 2020 was a severe economic setback, affecting Ireland in much the same way as other EU countries, and eliciting policies that were not dissimilar from those used elsewhere. But the rebound was quick. By 2022, employment was well above its pre-pandemic level, though the future prospects were clouded by the surge in inflation and the Ukraine war – imported energy price increases in particular causing a terms-of-trade loss comparable to that of the 1973 oil crisis.

Ireland has twice succumbed to macroeconomic mismanagement in the context of European exchange rate regimes. The resurgence of inflation during 2021–2 once more presents risks in this dimension, though here the role of European institutions is this time central.

That the departure of the UK from the EU would present challenges to the Irish economy will be evident from the examples we have seen of the close economic connections between Ireland and the UK. The complicated arrangements which have ensued from Brexit in maintaining the free movement of goods, services and people throughout the island of Ireland, and the associated uncertainty, have not been ideal, but the determination of Ireland's EU partners to protect Ireland's interests in this matter has been an impressive illustration of solidarity.

On a wider front, there are many other risks. Perhaps the largest of these comes from the fact that globalization, on which Ireland's economic advance has been built, has stalled and could, in some respects, go into reverse. This will enhance the relative importance of Europe in Ireland's international economic relations and could reduce the net benefits from the heavy reliance on US firms.

As Europe and the wider international community seek to reduce the degree to which large MNCs can avoid taxation on their profits, tax competition may increasingly be reined in, neutralizing what has been a vigorous policy instrument and increasingly important revenue source for Ireland.

Ireland can survive these shocks, but will need to pay continuous attention to maintaining its competitiveness and productivity within the Union. Complacency about the education system could impede the upgrading it needs to ensure the high-level skills (critical-analytical as well as scientific-technical) required in the modern economy. Foot-dragging over policies to combat environmental degradation and anthropogenic climate change cannot continue indefinitely, and the need to reduce greenhouse gas emissions will affect large parts of Irish agricultural production.

Ensuring resilience and efficiency, and arranging that the fruits of progress are fairly and inclusively shared, are matters which remain largely a national responsibility (for instance, housing, the legal system and healthcare). Housing in particular is a major and immediate constraint: the economy has outgrown its clothes because of the rapid growth in employment and population, exposing once again planning and policy weaknesses in this area.

Other aspects, including climate change and working conditions, need to be progressed within the EU, to which Ireland's commitment, albeit often shallow, has never been seriously challenged. How the Union evolves over the coming years, in terms of geopolitics as well as economics, will strongly influence Ireland's ability to achieve inclusive and stable prosperity.

Abbreviations

BMW	Border, Midland and Western Region
CAP	Common Agricultural Policy
CEE	Central and Eastern Europe
CIT	Compagnie Industrielle de Téléphone
CKD	completely knocked-down
CRH	Cement Roadstone Holdings
ECB	European Central Bank
EEC	European Economic Community
EFTA	European Free Trade Association
ELA	emergency liquidity assistance
EMS	European Monetary System
EMU	European Monetary Union
ERM	Exchange Rate Mechanism of the European Monetary System
ETS	Emissions Trading System
EU	European Union
EU15	The first 15 members of the EU
FDI	foreign direct investment
GB	Great Britain
GDP	gross domestic product
GFC	global financial crisis
GNI	gross national income
GNI*	modified gross national income (excluding distortions from MNCs)
GNP	gross national product
GPA	Guinness Peat Aviation
IDA	Industrial Development Authority
IFSC	Dublin International Financial Services Centre
IMF	International Monetary Fund
IPO	initial public offering (of equity shares)
IT	information technology
MNC	multinational corporation
MNE	multinational enterprise
NESC	National Economic and Social Council
OECD	Organization for Economic Co-operation and Development
OEEC	Organization for European Economic Co-operation

R&D	research and development
SEM	Single Electricity Market
TFR	total fertility rate
UK	United Kingdom
US	United States

References

Alesina, Alberto, Olivier Blanchard, Jordi Galí, Francesco Giavazzi and Harald Uhlig. 2001. *Defining a Macroeconomic Framework for the Euro Area* (London: Centre for Economic Policy Research).

Barrett, Alan, John FitzGerald and Brian Nolan. 2002. 'Earnings Inequality, Returns to Education and Immigration into Ireland'. *Labour Economics* 9: 665–80.

Barrett, Alan and Jean Goggin. 2010. 'Returning to the Question of a Wage Premium for Returning Migrants'. *National Institute Economic Review* 213 (1): R43–51.

Barrett, Alan, Íde Kearney and Yvonne McCarthy. 2007. *Quarterly Economic Commentary, Spring 2007* (Dublin: The Economic and Social Research Institute), pp. 1–35.

Barry, Frank. 2003. 'Economic Integration and Convergence Processes in the EU Cohesion Countries'. *Journal of Common Market Studies* 41(5): 897–921.

Barry, Frank. 2007. 'Third-Level Education, Foreign Direct Investment and Economic Boom in Ireland'. *International Journal of Technology Management* 38(3): 198–219.

Barry, Frank. 2011. 'Foreign Investment and the Politics of Export Profits Tax Relief 1956'. *Irish Economic and Social History* 38: 54–73.

Barry, Frank and Adele Bergin. 2019. 'Export Structure, FDI and the Rapidity of Ireland's Recovery from Crisis'. *The Economic and Social Review* 50(4): 707–24.

Barry, Frank, John Bradley and Aoife Hannan. 1999. 'The European Dimension: The Single Market and the Structural Funds'. In Frank Barry (ed.), *Understanding Ireland's Economic Growth* (London: Macmillan), pp. 99–118.

Bielenberg, Andy and Raymond Ryan. 2016. *An Economic History of Ireland since Independence* (London: Routledge).

Blackwell, John and Eoin O'Malley. 1984. 'The Impact of EEC Membership on Irish Industry'. In Patrick J. Drudy and Dermot McAleese (eds.), *Ireland and the European Community* (Cambridge: Cambridge University Press), pp. 107–44.

Bradley, John, John FitzGerald and Danny McCoy. 1991. *Medium-Term Review: 1991–1996* (Dublin: The Economic and Social Research Institute).

Bradley, John, Edgar Morgenroth and Gerhart Untiedt. 2003. 'Macro-regional Evaluation of the Structural Funds Using the HERMIN Modelling Framework'. *Italian Journal of Regional Science* 3(3): 5–28.

Brazys, Sam and Aidan Regan. 2021. 'Small States in Global Markets: The Political Economy of FDI-led Growth in Ireland'. In David Farrell and Niamh Hardiman (eds.), *Oxford Handbook of Irish Politics* (Oxford: Oxford University Press), pp. 405–22 .

Buckley, Peter J. and Frances Ruane. 2006. 'Foreign Direct Investment in Ireland: Policy Implications for Emerging Economies'. *The World Economy* 29(11): 1611–28.

Byrne, Elaine A. 2012. *Political Corruption in Ireland* (Manchester: Manchester University Press).

Cahill, Edward. 1997. *Corporate Financial Crisis in Ireland* (Dublin: Gill and Macmillan).

Campos, Nauro F., Fabrizio Coricelli and Luigi Moretti. 2019. 'Institutional Integration and Economic Growth in Europe'. *Journal of Monetary Economics* 103: 88–104.

Casey, Ciarán. 2022. *The History of the Department of Finance 1959–1999* (Dublin: Government Publications).

Crafts, Nicholas. 2014. 'Ireland's Medium-Term Growth Prospects: A Phoenix Rising?' *The Economic and Social Review* 45(1): 87–112.

Daly, Mary E. 2016. *Sixties Ireland* (Cambridge: Cambridge University Press).

Davies, Ronald B., Iulia Siedschlag and Zuzanna Studnicka. 2021. 'The Impact of Taxes on the Extensive and Intensive Margins of FDI'. *International Journal of Public Finance* 28(2): 434–64.

Dellepiane-Avellaneda, Sebastian, Niamh Hardiman and Jon Las Heras. 2021. 'Financial Resource Curse in the Eurozone Periphery'. *Review of International Political Economy* 29(4): 1287–313.

Department of Education. 1965. *Investment in Education* (Dublin: Stationery Office).

Duffy, David, John FitzGerald and Ide Kearney. 2005. 'Rising House Prices in an Open Labour Market'. *The Economic and Social Review* 36(3): 251–72.

Durkan, Joe, Doireann Fitzgerald and Colm Harmon. 1999. 'Education and Growth in the Irish Economy'. In Frank Barry (ed.), *Understanding Irish Economic Growth* (London: Macmillan), pp. 119–35.

Economic Statistics Review Group. 2016. *Report of the ESRG* (Dublin: Central Statistics Office). www.cso.ie/en/media/csoie/newsevents/documents/repor toftheeconomicstatisticsreviewgroup/Economic_Statistics_Review_(ESRG)_ Report_Dec_2016.pdf.

Everett, Mary M. 2015. 'Blowing the Bubble: The Global Funding of the Irish Credit Boom'. *The Economic and Social Review* 46(3): 339–65.

Fahey, Tony, John FitzGerald and Bertrand Maître. 1998. 'The Economic and Social Implications of Population Change'. *Journal of the Statistical and Social Inquiry Society of Ireland* 27(5): 185–222.

Fanning, Ronan. 1978. *The Irish Department of Finance 1922–58* (Dublin: Institute of Public Administration).

FitzGerald, John. 1998. 'An Irish Perspective on the Structural Funds'. *European Planning Studies* 6(6): 677–94.

FitzGerald, John. 1999. 'Wage Formation and the Labour Market', In Frank Barry (ed.), *Understanding Ireland's Economic Growth* (London: Macmillan), pp. 137–165.

FitzGerald, John. 2006. 'Lessons from 20 Years of Cohesion'. In Susanne Mundschenk, Michael Stierle, Ulrike Stierle-von Schutz and Iulia Traistaru (eds.), *Competitiveness and Growth in Europe: Lessons and Policy Implications for the Lisbon Strategy* (Cheltenham: Edward Elgar), pp. 65–99.

FitzGerald, John. 2012a. 'To Convergence and Beyond? Human Capital, Economic Adjustment and a Return to Growth'. ESRI Working Paper 419.

FitzGerald, John. 2012b. 'Restoring Credibility in Policy Making in Ireland'. *Public Money and Management* 32(1): 27–34.

FitzGerald, John. 2022a. 'National Accounts for a Global Economy: The Case of Ireland'. In Nadim Ahmad, Brent Moulton, J. David Richardson and Peter van de Ven (eds.), *The Challenges of Globalization in the Measurement of National Accounts* (Chicago: University of Chicago Press).

FitzGerald, John. 2022b. 'One Island, Two Labour Markets'. *Irish Studies in International Affairs* 33(2): 315–71.

FitzGerald, John, Íde Kearney, Edgar Morgenroth and Diarmaid Smyth. 1999. *National Investment Priorities for the Period 2000–2006* (Dublin: The Economic and Social Research Institute).

FitzGerald, John and Seán Kenny. 2018. 'Managing a Century of Debt'. *Journal of the Statistical and Social Inquiry Society of Ireland* 48: 1–40.

FitzGerald, John, Colm McCarthy, Edgar Morgenroth and Philip O'Connell. 2003. *The Mid-Term Evaluation of the National Development Plan and Community Support Framework for Ireland 2000–2006* (Dublin: The Economic and Social Research Institute).

FitzGerald, John and Edgar L. W. Morgenroth. 2020. 'The Northern Ireland Economy: Problems and Prospects'. *Journal of the Statistical and Social Inquiry Society of Ireland* 49: 64–84.

Fuchs-Schundeln, Nicola. 2019. 'Hours Worked Across the World: Facts and Driving Forces'. *National Institute Economic Review* 247(1): R3–18.

Garvin, Tom. 2005. *Preventing the Future: Why Was Ireland So Poor for So Long?* (Dublin: Gill).

Görg, Holger. 2000. 'Irish Direct Investment in the US: Evidence and Further Issues'. *Journal of the Statistical and Social Inquiry Society of Ireland* 30: 33–52.

Görg, Holger· and Frances Ruane. 1999. 'US Investment in EU Member Countries: The Internal Market and Sectoral Specialisation'. *Journal of Common Market Studies* 37(2): 333–48.

Gropp, Reint and Kristina Kostial. 2000. 'The Disappearing Tax Base: Is FDI Eroding Corporate Income Taxes?' IMF Working Paper 00/173.

Holton, Niamh and Donal O'Neill. 2017. 'The Changing Nature of Irish Wage Inequality from Boom to Bust'. *Economic and Social Review* 48(1): 1–26.

Honohan, Patrick. 1992. 'The Link between Irish and UK Unemployment'. *ESRI Quarterly Economic Commentary* Spring: 33–44.

Honohan, Patrick (ed.). 1997. *EU Structural Funds in Ireland: A Mid-term Evaluation of the CSF 1994–99* (Dublin: The Economic and Social Research Institute).

Honohan, Patrick. 1999. 'Fiscal Adjustment and Disinflation in Ireland: Setting the Basis for Economic Recovery and Expansion'. In Frank Barry (ed.), *Understanding Ireland's Economic Growth* (London: Macmillan), pp. 75–98.

Honohan, Patrick. 2019. *Currency, Credit and Crisis: Central Banking in Ireland and Europe* (Cambridge: Cambridge University Press).

Honohan, Patrick. 2021. 'Is Ireland Really the Most Prosperous Country in Europe?' *Economic Letter* 2021/1 (Dublin: Central Bank of Ireland).

Honohan, Patrick and Philip R. Lane. 2003. 'Divergent Inflation Rates in EMU'. *Economic Policy* 18(37): 357–94.

Honohan, Patrick and Gavin Murphy. 2010. 'Breaking the Sterling Link: Ireland's Decision to Enter the EMS'. Institute of International Integration Studies IIIS Trinity College Dublin Discussion Paper 317.

Honohan, Patrick and Brendan M. Walsh. 2002. 'Catching-Up with the Leaders: The Irish Hare'. *Brookings Papers on Economic Activity* 1: 1–79.

Jacobson, David. 1977. 'The Political Economy of Industrial Location: The Ford Motor Company at Cork, 1912–26'. *Irish Economic and Social History* 4: 36–55.

Jacobson, David and Bernadette Andreosso. 1990. 'Ireland as a Location for Multinational Investment'. In Michael Mulreany (ed.), *The Single European Market and the Irish Economy* (Dublin: Institute of Public Administration), pp. 307–34.

Kearney, Ide. 2012. 'Measuring Fiscal Stance'. *ESRI Quarterly Economic Commentary* Autumn: 67–88.

Kearney, Ide, Danny McCoy, David Duffy, Michael McMahon and Diarmaid Smyth. 2000. 'Assessing the Stance of Irish Fiscal Policy'. In Alan Barrett (ed.), *Budget Perspectives* (Dublin: The Economic and Social Research Institute), pp. 1–37.

Laffan, Brigid. 2021. 'Ireland in a European Context'. In David Farrell and Niamh Hardiman (eds.), *Oxford Handbook of Irish Politics* (Oxford: Oxford University Press), pp. 127–44.

Laffan, Brigid and Jane O'Mahony. 2008. *Ireland and the European Union* (Basingstoke: Palgrave Macmillan).

Lane, Philip R. 2015. 'The Funding of the Irish Domestic Banking System During the Boom'. *Journal of the Statistical and Social Inquiry Society of Ireland* 44: 40–65.

Lawless, Martina. 2019. 'Firms and Trade on the Island of Ireland'. *Journal of the Statistical and Social Inquiry Society of Ireland* 48: 211–21.

Lawless, Martina, J. Peter Neary and Zuzanna Studnicka. 1999. 'South-North Trade in Ireland: Gravity and Firms from the Good Friday Agreement to Brexit'. *The Economic and Social Review* 50(4): 751–66.

Lee, Joseph. 1989. *Ireland 1912–85* (Cambridge: Cambridge University Press).

MacCarthaigh, Muiris and Niamh Hardiman. 2020. 'Exploiting Conditionality: EU and International Actors and Post-NPM Reform in Ireland'. *Public Policy and Administration* 35(2): 179–200.

MacSharry, Ray and Padraic A. White. 2000. *The Making of the Celtic Tiger: The Insider Story of Ireland's Boom Economy* (Dublin: Mercier Press).

Madden, David. 2014. 'Winners and Losers on the Roller-Coaster: Ireland, 2003–2011'. *The Economic and Social Review* 45(3): 405–21.

McAleese, Dermot. 1971. *Effective Tariffs and the Structure of Industrial Production in Ireland* (Dublin: The Economic and Social Research Institute).

McCoy, Danny. 1991. 'Macroeconomic Impact of Environmental Policy on Acid Rain'. In John Bradley, John FitzGerald and Danny McCoy (eds.), *Medium-Term Review: 1991–1996* (Dublin: The Economic and Social Research Institute), pp. 91–101.

Mitchell, Tara and Francis O'Toole. 2021. 'Regulatory Policy'. In John O'Hagan, Francis O'Toole and Ciara Whelan (eds.), *The Economy of Ireland* (London: Red Globe Press), pp. 109–35.

Murphy, Mary P. 2015. 'Forty Years of EU Influencing Social Policy in Ireland: A Glass Half Full?' *Administration* 62: 69–86.

Neary, J. Peter and Cormac Ó Gráda. 1991. 'Protection, Economic War and Structural Change: The 1930s in Ireland'. *Irish Historical Studies* 27(107): 250–66.

Newbery, David, Horst Siebert and John Vickers. 1990. 'Acid Rain'. *Economic Policy* 5(11): 297–346.

Nolan, Brian and Bertrand Maître. 2000. 'Income Inequality'. In Brian Nolan, Philip J. O'Connell and Christopher T. Whelan (eds.), *Bust to Boom: The Irish Experience of Growth and Inequality* (Dublin: Institute of Public Administration), pp. 147–62.

Ó Cinnéide, Seamus. 2010. 'From Poverty to Social Inclusion: The EU and Ireland'. In Philip O'Connor and Anna Visser (eds.), *Ireland and the European Social Inclusion Strategy: Lessons Learned and the Road Ahead* (Dublin: European Anti Poverty Network Ireland), pp. 18–36.

O'Donoghue, Cathal. 2022. 'A Century of Agriculture: A Policy-Driven Sector'. *Journal of the Statistical and Social Inquiry Society of Ireland* forthcoming.

Ó Gráda, Cormac. 1997. *A Rocky Road: The Irish Economy since the 1920s* (Manchester: Manchester University Press).

Ó Gráda, Cormac. 2002. 'Is the Celtic Tiger a Paper Tiger?' *ESRI Quarterly Economic Commentary* Spring: 51–62.

Ó Gráda, Cormac and Kevin Hjortshøj O'Rourke. 2022. 'The Irish Economy During the Century after Partition'. *The Economic History Review* 75(2): 336–70.

Oireachtas. 2016. *Report of the Joint Committee of Inquiry into the Banking Crisis* (Dublin: Stationery Office). https://inquiries.oireachtas.ie/banking.

O'Leary, Eoin. 2015. *Irish Economic Development: High-Performing EU State or Serial Underachiever* (London: Routledge).

O'Malley, Eoin. 1989. *Industry and Economic Development* (Dublin: Gill and Macmillan).

O'Rourke, Kevin and Jeffrey Williamson. 1999. *Globalization and History* (Cambridge, MA: MIT Press).

O'Rourke, Kevin Hjortshøj. 2017. 'Independent Ireland in Comparative Perspective'. *Irish Economic and Social History* 44(1): 19–45.

O'Toole, Fintan. 2021. *We Don't Know Ourselves* (London: Head of Zeus).

Oxford University Centre for Business Taxation. 2017. *CBT Tax Database.* https://oxfordtax.sbs.ox.ac.uk/cbt-tax-database (consulted 16 July 2022).

Perotti, Roberto. 2013. 'The "Austerity Myth": Gain without Pain?' In Alberto Alesina and Francesco Giavazzi (eds.), *Fiscal Policy after the Financial Crisis* (Chicago: University of Chicago Press), pp. 307–54.

Roantree, Barra, Bertrand Maître, Alyvia McTague and Ivan Privalko. 2021. *Poverty, Income Inequality and Living Standards in Ireland* (Dublin: The Economic and Social Research Institute).

Romalis, John. 2007. 'Capital Taxes, Trade Costs and the Irish Miracle'. *Journal of the European Economic Association* 5(2–3): 459–69.

Ruane, Frances and Holger Görg. 1996. 'Aspects of Foreign Direct Investment in Irish Manufacturing since 1973: Policy and Performance'. *Journal of the Statistical and Social Inquiry Society of Ireland* 27: 37–93.

Ruane, Frances and Holger Görg. 1997. 'The Impact of Foreign Direct Investment on Sectoral Adjustment in the Irish Economy'. *National Institute Economic Review* 160(1): 76–86.

Ruane, Frances and Holger Görg. 2000. 'European Integration and Peripherality: Lessons from the Irish Experience'. *The World Economy* 23 (3): 405–21.

Ruane, Frances, Iulia Siedschlag and Gavin Murphy. 2014. 'Globalization and Ireland's Export Performance'. In Louis Brennan (ed.), *Enacting Globalization* (London: Palgrave Macmillan), pp. 205–18. https://doi.org/10 .1057/9781137361943_19.

Ruane, Frances and Julie Sutherland. 2005. 'Export Performance and Destination Characteristics of Irish Manufacturing Industry'. *Review of World Economics* 141: 442–59.

Ruane, Frances and Ali Uğur. 2010. 'Foreign Direct Investment and Productivity Spillovers in Irish Manufacturing Industry: Evidence from Plant Level Panel Data'. *International Journal of the Economics of Business* 12(1): 53–66.

Ryan, W. J. Louden. 1949. 'The Nature and Effect of Protective Policy in Ireland'. PhD Thesis. University of Dublin.

Siedschlag, Iulia, Mattia Di Ubaldo and Manuel Tong Koecklin, 2017. *Comparative Performance of Indigenous and Multinational Firms Operating in Ireland* (Dublin: The Economic and Social Research Institute).

Siedschlag, Iulia and Manual Tong Koecklin. 2019. *The Impact of the UK's EU Exit on the Attractiveness of Northern Ireland to FDI and Associated Job Creation Effects* (Belfast: Northern Ireland Department for the Economy).

Siedschlag, Iulia, Xiaoheng Zhang and Donal Smith. 2013. 'What Determines the Location Choice of Multinational Firms in the Information and Communication Technologies Sector?' *Economics of Innovation and New Technology* 22(6): 581–600.

Tørsløv, Thomas, Ludvig Wier and Gabriel Zucman. 2022. 'The Missing Profits of Nations'. *The Review of Economic Studies* forthcoming.

Voitchovsky, Sarah, Bertrand Maître and Brian Nolan. 2012. 'Wage Inequality in Ireland's "Celtic Tiger" Boom'. *The Economic and Social Review* 43(1): 99–133.

Walsh, Brendan M. 1974. 'Expectations, Information, and Human Migration: Specifying an Econometric Model of Irish Migration to Britain'. *Journal of Regional Science* 14(1): 107–21.

Acknowledgements

This Element distils knowledge that has been gleaned by the authors over the years from oral and written sources – teachers, colleagues and friends – too numerous to mention. Specific thanks are due to Frank Barry, Frank Convery, Niamh Hardiman, Iseult Honohan, Íde Kearney, Philip Lane, Brian Nolan, Cormac Ó Gráda, Frances Ruane and two anonymous referees for suggestions and comments.

Cambridge Elements ≡

Economics of European Integration

Nauro F. Campos

University College London

Nauro F. Campos is Professor of Economics at University College London and Research Professor at ETH-Zürich. His main fields of interest are political economy and European integration. He has previously taught at CERGE-EI (Prague), California (Fullerton), Newcastle, Brunel, Bonn, Paris 1 Sorbonne and Warwick. He was a visiting Fulbright Fellow at Johns Hopkins (Baltimore), a Robert McNamara Fellow at The World Bank, and a CBS Fellow at Oxford. He is currently a Research Fellow at IZA-Bonn, a Professorial Fellow at UNU-MERIT (Maastricht University), a member of the Scientific Advisory Board of the (Central) Bank of Finland, and a Senior Fellow of the ESRC Peer Review College. He was a visiting scholar at the University of Michigan, ETH, USC, Bonn, UCL, Stockholm, IMF, World Bank, and the European Commission. From 2009 to 2014, he was seconded as Senior Economic Advisor/SRF to the Chief Economist of the UK's Department for International Development. He received his Ph.D. from the University of Southern California (Los Angeles) in 1997, where he was lucky enough to learn about institutions from Jeff Nugent and Jim Robinson and (more than) happy to be Dick Easterlin's RA. He is the editor in chief of *Comparative Economic Studies*, the journal of the Association for Comparative Economic Studies.

About the Series

This Element series provides authoritative, up-to-date reviews of core topics and recent developments in the field with particular emphasis on structural, policy and political economy issues. State-of-the-art contributions explore topics such as labour mobility, the euro crisis, Brexit, immigration, inequality, international trade, unemployment, climate change policy, and more.

Printed in the United States
by Baker & Taylor Publisher Services